T0309803

Managing Client Emotions in Forensic Accounting and Fraud Investigation

Founded in 1807, John Wiley & Sons is the oldest independent publishing company in the United States. With offices in North America, Europe, Asia, and Australia, Wiley is globally committed to developing and marketing print and electronic products and services for our customers' professional and personal knowledge and understanding.

The Wiley Corporate F&A series provides information, tools, and insights to corporate professionals responsible for issues affecting the profitability of their company, from accounting and finance to internal controls and performance management.

For a list of available titles, visit our Web site at www.WileyFinance.com.

Managing Client Emotions in Forensic Accounting and Fraud Investigation

STEPHEN PEDNEAULT

WILEY

Published by John Wiley & Sons, Inc., Hoboken, New Jersey.
Published simultaneously in Canada.

For general information on our other products and services or for technical support, please contact our Customer Care Department within the United States at (800) 762-2974, outside the United States at (317) 572-3993 or fax (317) 572-4002.

Wiley also publishes its books in a variety of electronic formats. Some content that appears in print may not be available in electronic formats. For more information about Wiley products, visit our web site at www.wiley.com.

Library of Congress Cataloging-in-Publication Data is Available:

ISBN: 9781119471493(hardback)
ISBN: 9781119473657(epdf)
ISBN: 9781119473565(epub)

Cover Design: Wiley
Cover Image: © Pressmaster / Shutterstock
SKY10027933_070221

To Kim, Justin, and Evan. I trust you miss the table in the center
of the room as much as I do.
Dad

Contents

Preface

WHEN YOU PICKED UP this book, you most likely found the title to be unique from the other fraud material and books available. You might have asked yourself: Why would someone write a book about client emotions within the context of fraud investigations?

Well, the short answer is this: It has never been done before. The long answer is that emotions play a crucial role in the unfolding of fraud investigations. In this book, you will discover how intertwined client emotions become with the fraud examination process.

Even if you have significant experience in the fraud field, you may not realize how important addressing client emotions is in successfully resolving a fraud matter. You may think that fraud examiners, forensic accountants, and financial investigators should focus their expertise on accounting, numbers, electronic records, transactions, and other similar aspects of a case, leaving the issue of emotions to other more qualified professionals, such as psychologists and social workers. Well, that is certainly a valid position, and there is certainly a role for qualified counseling and psychology professionals to help the individuals involved in a fraud case. However, based on my 31 years of experience as a forensic accountant and fraud examiner, I have found that fraud examiners cannot avoid addressing client emotions in nearly every interaction during an engagement.

My clients and referral sources have come to expect me to be not only a forensic accountant, tax expert, auditor, strategist, technology expert, interviewer, and investigator, but also a social worker and psychologist. I attribute my career success to my ability to wear all these hats while providing my services.

As I've reflected back on my career, I've tried to identify the unique approaches that have set me apart from others in my field and allowed me to succeed in my engagements. I identified four major factors crucial to my success: (1) my ability to receive referrals for future engagements based on my reputation and experience; (2) the passion I bring to work each and every day; (3) my ability to provide superior customer service, even outside of normal business hours; and (4) my proficiency in networking and relationship building.

However, while each of those attributes has played a critical role in my success, the number-one factor that truly differentiates my approach from others is how I treat the individuals involved in my matters – whether they be victims, attorneys, suspects, witnesses, family members, or coworkers.

In a fraud investigation, the important deliverables are determining the facts, identifying the person responsible, and holding the culprit accountable for their actions. However, my firm also focuses on bringing closure to the parties involved.

There is nothing magical in what I have accomplished in my career. The two things I have learned to do well in every engagement are to listen and to care. Surprisingly, listening and caring have played a much larger role in earning the respect of my clients than anything else I've accomplished in an engagement. I believe this is because – sadly – few people today focus their business approach and services on these basic needs.

If you listen to clients and care about them, you will succeed. Add passion to the equation, and your career and reputation will skyrocket. Mine did.

Acknowledgments

TO MY FAMILY WHO stood by me along this journey, an endeavor I believe we all thought would never get accomplished, and one that I am extremely grateful for its completion.

To Jaime DeBlanc-Knowles of Fresh Ink, for all of her editing assistance and guidance that she provided me, adjusting her schedule to accommodate this project, and delivering nothing but prompt and professional responses that transformed my writing.

To all the folks at Wiley who have been nothing but patient with me, allowing me to complete this project while I was working through some difficult issues impacting my vision.

To all of my clients over many, many years who had a decision to make when seeking the assistance of a fraud professional, and chose to allow me and my firm to assist them in resolving their matters.

To all my friends and colleagues at the University of Connecticut, School of Business, Master of Science in Accounting (MSA) program. I not only love working in this field, I also love teaching students about it, and I have all of you to thank for allowing me the opportunity to teach in your program. Go Huskies!

And to all of the fraud professionals working in this field, and those thinking of joining it. I hope that you bring passion and professionalism to every engagement, and your career is successful and rewarding. It has been for me.

About the Author

STEPHEN PEDNEAULT, CPA/CFF, CFE, is the principal of Forensic Accounting Services, LLC, a local CPA firm in Manchester, Connecticut, specializing in forensic accounting, litigation support, and fraud-related matters.

Working in public accounting for 31 years, Steve is a certified public accountant, certified in financial forensics, and a certified fraud examiner. He has an associate's degree in criminal justice from Manchester Community College and a bachelor's degree in accounting from Eastern Connecticut State University, where he graduated summa cum laude.

Through his investigative work, Steve has examined frauds ranging from a few thousand dollars to amounts into the millions. His expertise also lies in preventing and investigating embezzlements and other financial frauds in a wide range of contexts. Steve has been disclosed in matters many times as an expert, and has testified at deposition and at trial.

As an adjunct faculty member at the University of Connecticut, Steve authored an innovative course on forensic accounting and fraud examination that has been offered since 2008 as an online class within UConn's Master of Science in Accounting (MSA) program.

When Steve is not playing detective and finding missing money, he enjoys spending time with his family, especially biking and hiking. In addition, Steve has volunteered as an EMT on a community ambulance service for over 25 years. He also contributes his time in support of Boy Scout Troop 25 of Manchester, Connecticut, where both of his boys earned the rank of Eagle Scout.

Steve has authored four other books published by Wiley: *Fraud 101*; *Anatomy of a Fraud Investigation*; *A Practical Guide to Preventing and Detecting Employee Theft and Embezzlement*; and *Forensic Accounting and Fraud Investigation for Non-Experts* (co-authored with Frank Rudewicz).

Introduction

THIS BOOK AIMS TO educate readers about the wide range of emotions encountered in nearly every fraud engagement, while also providing tips and strategies for dealing with those emotions. My goal is to share examples of cases I've been involved in throughout my 30-plus years in the industry and illustrate how client emotions come into play.

I am not a psychologist or social worker, nor do I profess to have expertise in these areas. I am simply an experienced CPA specializing in forensic accounting and fraud-related matters who is willing to share what I have learned over many years.

Since there are many different contexts for fraud and financial crime, there are also many different job descriptions and titles for those who provide services in these areas. Professionals working in these fields can include fraud examiners, forensic accountants, public accountants, auditors, internal auditors, financial investigators, police officers, agents, and other investigators, as well as attorneys, prosecutors, and defense counsel. In order to use one consistent term in my discussions, I refer to the individual working in this field as a *fraud examiner*.

I have also used generic terminology to refer to the other actors in a fraud investigation. Individuals encountered during fraud engagements include not only victims but also suspects, witnesses, family members, spouses, friends, and business associates. Throughout my book, I often refer to "client" emotions, but the term *client* is meant to encompass anyone involved in the engagement, not just the individual or organization for whom the fraud examiner performs fraud-related services.

Finally, a fraud investigation can be referred to by many names: a fraud examination, a fraud case, a fraud matter, or a fraud engagement. While the terminology may differ, each name refers to the same basic concept – a type of fraud scenario that requires the services of a fraud examiner. In my book, I use the terms *case*, *matter*, and *engagement* interchangeably.

Regardless of the terminology and context, fraud examiners serve the same basic but important purpose of determining the facts of a matter – the *who, what, where, when, how, how long, how much,* and other factual details. Today, a significant number of resources are available to teach both new and experienced fraud examiners how to perform fraud engagements, conduct interviews, collect and maintain evidence, write reports, testify at deposition and trial, and everything in between. However, a fraud examiner would be hard-pressed to locate any resources that train them on how to address client emotions during fraud examinations.

In my experience, in nearly every fraud matter the fraud examiner will encounter a wide range of client emotions, from rage to denial to depression. Dealing with client emotions can be challenging at times, and conducting fraud engagements without addressing the emotions of the different parties involved hampers progress. Choosing to embrace rather than ignore clients' emotions can often make the difference between successfully resolving a matter or allowing it to continue in perpetuity.

Every fraud examiner should seek out training in this area and develop practical strategies he or she can use for dealing with client emotions. There is a pressing need to discuss this aspect of fraud investigation and forensic accounting with individuals entering the field, as well as those with minimal experience. Even experienced individuals will benefit from witnessing how the success of an engagement often hinges on how fraud examiners address client emotions.

The discussions in the following chapters are based on my 31 years of experience working as a certified public accountant (CPA), specializing as a certified fraud examiner (CFE) conducting fraud investigations and forensic accounting engagements. Working in the context of public accounting, I have mainly been brought into client situations from the outside, rather than working internally within an organization or for a governmental agency. Thus, while many of the discussions apply to any context, fraud examiners may have to adapt them to their particular context.

I truly hope you can learn a thing or two from my experiences and apply this knowledge in your fraud examinations.

And to those experienced fraud examiners, I trust you will be nodding along as you read my stories, as you too have had many similar experiences in your own client matters.

Enjoy the read.

PART ONE

Why Address
Client Emotions?

CHAPTER ONE

Encountering Client Emotions

 EVERY CLIENT HAS A STORY

Every fraud engagement starts with a story. It is critical that the fraud examiner obtain this story, knowing there are at least three versions to be had: the version provided by the party retaining the fraud examiner; the version provided by opposing parties, such as the individual suspected of committing fraud; and the truth. As more parties are added to the matter, the number of versions increases, but in the end there is only one version that matters: the truth.

In order to start off my discussions about client emotions, I will start with a story. Sadly, I have seen many similar stories, and this one is a great example of how client emotions become intertwined with a fraud examination.

I received a phone call from an attorney who was calling about a potential fraud matter. After briefly introducing himself, the attorney explained that he represented a sister and brother regarding an estate matter. His clients' mother had died a year earlier, and as part of the mother's estate planning, her assets had been designated to go directly into a trust. The brother and sister were the sole beneficiaries of the trust, sharing an equal inheritance. However, the attorney had found it difficult to obtain any information from the trustee, and his clients believed the trustee had mishandled their mother's estate and trust. Although funds were available for distribution to the attorney's clients, to date they had received nothing from the estate or trust.

I set up a time to meet at the attorney's office to review the records and information he had been able to collect, as well as to meet his clients. The attorney ended our conversation by warning me that the sister was very emotional and her brother had a serious drinking problem and could become hostile.

When the day of our meeting arrived, I drove to the attorney's office with one of my staff members. We were greeted at the door and brought into an empty office where the attorney met with us privately prior to introducing us to his clients. He said he had been meeting with the sister and brother for an hour or so and that the brother had become quite agitated toward the trustee. The attorney warned us again that the brother could be a bit of a loose cannon.

Next, the attorney brought us into his conference room, where the sister and brother were sitting at the table. The sister, a well-dressed, mild-looking woman with a petite frame, sat next her brother, a middle-aged man dressed in jeans, a flannel button-down shirt, and sneakers. She was sitting upright and attentive, with papers neatly stacked in front of her, while he was slouched back in his chair at a 45-degree angle. The attorney introduced us to the siblings, and we started the meeting.

The attorney provided his rendition of what had happened from the time the siblings' mother had died to the present, identifying the difficulties he had encountered in obtaining information and answers for his clients. As part of his story, the attorney noted that the mother was divorced from his clients' father, who had since died, and that she had remarried a man named Tim. That made Tim his clients' stepfather, although his clients were well into their fifties when their mother remarried.

Sometime between the mother's marriage to Tim and her death, their mother had redone her estate planning, changing the terms, beneficiaries, and distributions, which had previously been a simple estate left solely to her son and daughter. The new estate planning designated all of the mother's assets to be transferred into a trust for the benefit of her son and daughter. The mother named her accountant as the independent trustee over her trust and provided him with broad authority over the management and use of her trust's assets until Tim's death. Upon Tim's death, the trustee was to distribute the remaining trust assets to the son and daughter.

The trust provided two additional provisions. First, during Tim's lifetime, the trustee was to distribute a specified amount each calendar year to the son and daughter. Second, the trustee was to allow Tim the exclusive use of the mother's residence until his death, with the provision that the trustee had the right to inspect the property at any time, provided he gave Tim advance notice of the inspection.

So far, the scenario the attorney described was similar to many we had seen in previous matters, and we predicted that the story would identify a difficult trustee and clashes between the brother, the sister, the trustee, and Tim.

The trustee, who was retirement-aged, was a certified public accountant (CPA), as was his son, who was 20 years his junior. The son was also an independent investment manager, and his father chose to utilize his son to manage the trust's investments. The clients' attorney said he had requested statements from both the father and the son regarding the trust assets and investments, but to date neither had produced any information.

The clients' attorney stated that Tim had been living in the mother's house prior to her death and had continued living there even after she became sick and relocated to a nursing home. Tim still lived in the house, and the brother and sister had heard through neighbors that Tim had let the house and yard become run down. Tim was dealing with significant health issues, and it was uncertain how long he would live.

When the attorney finally ended his story, he allowed his clients to speak for the first time since the meeting had started.

The sister spoke first, thanking us for meeting today. She took out her notebook and read through her notes and timeline as she added more detail to the attorney's story. The sister said she'd had a very close relationship with her mother up until the time her mother met Tim. Once Tim came into the picture, however, their relationship became strained, and it did not return to its former closeness until the last days of her mother's life. She said that her mother had been physically and emotionally abused by Tim and had twice been treated at the hospital for injuries Tim inflicted. However, her mother would not leave Tim and returned to him after each incidence of violence. The sister stated that, even when her mother had cancer, Tim continued to abuse and neglect her. The last time her mother had been hospitalized, she had appeared malnourished. The sister said that her mother had told her that she was afraid of Tim and that she did not want to go home.

During her account, the sister's face turned red and her eyes puffy. Tears streamed down her face.

The sister said that Tim had come to the nursing home and created a scene, which led to her obtaining a restraining order to keep Tim away from her mother. Even as her mother lay in bed dying at the nursing home, her mother feared Tim would come there, and thus she never relaxed. Her mother told her that she was so sorry Tim had interfered with her and her daughter's prior relationship. The mother felt that the last few years of her life had been her worst, as she had suffered abuse, neglect, illness, and separation from her children. The sister had not known how bad things were between her mother and Tim, and it broke her heart to sit talking with her dying mother, knowing she couldn't fix the past and had little to no time left to make her mother happy again.

After this disclosure, the sister broke down and cried, but received no comfort from her brother. After a few minutes, the sister apologized for crying and described how angry she was with Tim and the trustee, whom she described as working with Tim to take the estate and trust funds for themselves. Her face tightened, and her fists clenched. She said that both Tim and the trustee were crooks, as was the trustee's investor son, and that she wanted them all removed from anything to do with her mother's estate and trust. She wanted them all locked up in prison. She wished Tim was dead because of what he had done to her mother. Every day that Tim lived in her mother's house and the trustee continued to handle the funds, she said, more and more money would be improperly spent or stolen by them, leaving less for her brother and herself.

Then, the sister turned to her brother and asked if he wanted to add anything to the story. The brother's face tensed, and he also clenched his fists. He rapidly shifted from slouching to sitting upright in his chair. The brother shouted that Tim should be dead for what he'd done to his mother and for what he continued to do, living at his mother's house, which rightfully belonged to them. He said that he had gone to the house on a few occasions and recognized that Tim was nothing but a drunk. Tim was overweight, poorly dressed, and in poor health. The house and yard were in a state of major disrepair, even though there was evidence the trustee had paid funds to maintain the house.

The brother was clearly angry, his face bright red. He said that if Tim were to die, the trustee could be ordered to close out the estate and trust, and he and his sister could go on with their lives and find closure after their mother's death. He said he did not have a permanent address or mailing address and that he lived for long periods of time in remote areas where mail was not important. He was leaving for the mountains of Maine right after our meeting, and we might never see him again. He might connect with his sister so she knew where to reach him, mainly to know when the trust distributions were available. If he had the option, he would handle Tim, the trustee, and the trustee's son *his way*. That way, he could get closure for his sister, who could then move on with her life and not have to deal with Tim or the trustee in the future.

The brother understood that the estate and trust had to be handled through attorneys and the probate court, because that was how these things got resolved civilly. However, he said, it was just going to cost more time and much more money, and the three men, especially Tim, would likely never face any genuine consequences for their actions. The brother ended by saying it would be best if he were to go far away and disappear into the woods so that he wouldn't do anything rash. The brother rose from his seat, punched the table, and then threw open the conference room door and went down the hallway toward the exit. We watched him light up a cigarette on the rear lawn beyond the parking lot.

The sister said her brother tended to get very angry, especially when he hadn't been drinking. Most of the time he was drunk; however, today he appeared sober, or at least less drunk than usual. She said that when her brother got angry like this, he needed alone time, since nothing could be said or done to calm him down. She said he would return to the meeting when he was ready, likely after a few cigarettes and perhaps a drink from something he had stashed away on his person. She said we had nothing to fear from him, since his anger was directed toward Tim, the trustee, and the trustee's son, not us. Her brother had not visited much during their mother's last few years. He was often gone without contact for months at a time. She said it was best for her brother to leave again for a while so that he didn't act on his anger.

We recognized that our meeting was far from over. This was just an intermission. Up until that moment, all we had obtained was their stories about why we had been called to this meeting. We still needed to determine how to proceed, what services we were to perform, and how our work would help the attorney resolve the estate and trust matters, bringing them the closure they so badly needed. These issues needed to be discussed today, before the brother went missing again.

The meeting provided good insight into the sister and brother's characters – and into the emotions we would likely encounter as we worked to help resolve their matter.

In the course of working on this matter over the subsequent year, we never heard from the brother again. We dealt mainly with the sister and her attorneys. We met with the sister a dozen times and spoke to her at times almost daily. She was frustrated by the delays she encountered and angered by the fact that nothing was happening while the funds continued to be diminished month after month. We were there to listen and help her work through the issues until her case was resolved.

In time, through aggressive efforts by the sister's new attorney, the fiduciaries were removed, the attorney for the fiduciaries was ordered to return the excess fees they had paid to themselves, and the siblings were finally able to receive the remains of their inheritance. The sister sent us a handwritten letter expressing her appreciation for our support throughout the ordeal, and attributed our involvement as the one factor that had prevented her from going insane during the pendency of her matter. ▪

A case like this illustrates how client emotions are inseparable from the facts of the fraud engagement. When dealing with these types of cases, fraud examiners should recognize that fraud, like any other type of crime, is very personal to the victim, and clients can become very emotional as they work through the process toward resolving their matter.

Clients want to tell their story. My advice is: Let them. Set up an in-person meeting, clear your schedule, and prepare to be their audience. They will provide details about their lives that have nothing to do with the present matter, such as issues they experienced during childhood, family relationships, breakups, disappointments, financial strains, pets, and more. They feel the details are important, so let them tell their story on their terms. Listen and take notes. Ask questions to clarify things, but try to keep your interruptions to a minimum. At some level, the client telling you their full story is therapy for them.

Either they will eventually get to the point in discussing the present matter or, once they feel they have provided you with all the details, they will stop talking. This moment is when you can guide them to discussing the present matter – the reason they need your services. It is important that, even if you make this transition for them by focusing them on the issue at hand, you do not make them feel as if the details they have provided up to that point have been unimportant or irrelevant. Recognize that it is all important and relevant to them.

Often, clients will ask you what you think of all of the details they provided. It is critical for you to be genuine, objective, and respectful, regardless of how irrelevant those details may seem. Building a rapport with clients starts with listening to their story, and sometimes the little details that appeared irrelevant in the beginning can prove useful later in the fraud examination.

In the end, every fraud examiner wants to know the same two things – why the individual needs a fraud examiner and what the individual hopes will be accomplished by using a fraud examiner. To that end, the examiner may be tempted to borrow an approach from the 1950s series *Dragnet*: "Just the facts, ma'am." That's certainly an approach I understand: *Just tell me why you called my firm and what you hope we can do to help you resolve your matter. Let's keep this meeting as brief as possible.* However, I have found that that approach is simply not effective in reality.

My experience has shown me that, as much as I may want to surgically extract the pertinent facts and keep irrelevant conversation to a minimum, that strategy is not successful in helping to resolve the client's matter. It's far more effective to take a little extra time to listen to their full story.

Listening to clients' stories will not be limited to that first interaction. I use every interaction as an opportunity to interview the individual. Some interviews are more formal than others, but if I approach every one as an opportunity to learn more information, I may discover details that were omitted in previous meetings, which will only help me in my fact-finding process. Sometimes, a subsequent opportunity to ask questions and listen to a client's responses has led to my discovering details of other activities that I'd known nothing about up to that point. This proved to be the case in the following engagement.

We were working with counsel on a matter involving a school finance manager who appeared to be stealing funds from the school. Families were sending tuition and other payments to the school, but the funds were not reaching the school's bank accounts. Although the school's enrollment was strong, the school was in poor financial health, and its reserve funding was depleted.

We scheduled a time to meet with the finance manager at the school, gain an understanding of the school's finances, and obtain access to all the financial records, including bank statements, paid invoices, and deposit details. When we arrived, a very nervous administrative employee who worked with the finance manager met with us. She said the finance manager had not come to work as planned, and that if we wanted to meet with the finance manager, we would have to reschedule for another day. It was obvious that the woman was nervous, as well as caught in a difficult position, since her supervisor hadn't provided any notice or explanation for her absence. We used the interaction to provide the administrative employee with assurances that we simply needed her help and the fact that the finance manager had not shown up was in no way a reflection on the administrative employee. We then sat down with her to gain a general understanding of the school's finances, systems, and operations. In other words, we started to establish a rapport with her.

Seeing that we were at the school and had not received notice of the finance manager's absence, we assumed that the finance manager must have realized her illegal actions were about to be uncovered. She would avoid meeting with us and having to explain her actions, buying herself perhaps a few more days. (It turned out we were right: The finance manager's unauthorized diversion of funds was uncovered, and she was ultimately held accountable for her thefts.) However, the goal in our initial meeting was not to reveal any of this to the administrative employee. We needed her to help us, so we needed to minimize – in her mind – our involvement in this matter.

While we were at the school, we had the administrative employee identify the location of the financial records, including the bank statements.

The administrative employee showed us to the file cabinets and told us that the bank statements were all maintained offsite. We asked her how many bank accounts there were, and she said there were many. We asked her why the bank statements were kept offsite. She couldn't explain to us why they were not maintained in the file cabinets with the school's other financial records. She said that most of the accounts were maintained by the finance manager, but that there were other smaller accounts maintained by other individuals involved in the school. We created a list of these accounts and identified the individual associated with each account's records.

We collected two years' worth of financial records from the file cabinets and secured them in our cars to transport them to our offices for safekeeping. We thanked the administrative employee for her help and told her how much we appreciated her helping us find the financial records.

We then asked the administrative employee to contact anyone who maintained any of the school's bank account information or any other type of school financial records and instruct them to bring all those records to the school the next day – 24 hours from that point. The administrative employee could tell each person that auditors were looking for the school's financial records and needed to have the statements and records back at the school to continue their audit. We told her we would return tomorrow to retrieve the bank records. Once again, we told her that we really appreciated her help and we looked forward to meeting with her again tomorrow. At that point, she seemed much more relaxed than when we'd first met her.

The next day, when we returned to the school, the administrative employee told us that the finance manager had not come to work again, but that she had dropped off a box of bank statements in her office. The finance manager must have come to the office after school hours and left the box on her desk. The administrative employee had gone through the box that morning, sorted the statements by bank account, and organized them for us. She also told us that others had brought their account statements to her that morning, and she had those records organized as well.

We took out the list of accounts we had created with her the day before and asked her if statements for all of the accounts she'd identified had been received. She said that they all had, except for one. When we asked her what account it was, she said it was a sports account, which the athletic coach and his wife managed from their house. We asked her if she had requested that the coach bring all of the statements to her at the school this morning. She said she had, but that she hadn't yet received anything. We then asked her to tell us about the sports program and the coach.

She said that the coach and his family had been running the sports program at the school for many, many years. She said that they handled the account on their own, receiving their statements directly at their house and taking care of their own deposits and payments. She said that her office really had nothing to do with the sports account, and it had been that way as long as she had been at the school – some 10 or more years – and that she didn't think there was a lot of activity involved with the sports account.

She said that families paid for their children to participate in the various sports teams and programs and that the costs associated with those programs were paid from the sports fees collected. We asked her what the coach and his family were like, where they lived, and what she knew about them. She said they lived right around the corner, in a house not far from the school, and as far as she knew, this was the coach's only job. She said the family had two children who attended the school (tuition-free, since they were school employees). She said she believed the coach's wife had a job, but did not know what she did or where she worked. She thought the coach had obtained a credit card in the school's name to use with the sports program, but she had never seen any of the credit card statements.

She seemed to be getting nervous again, and she asked us if the coach was in trouble. We told her it wasn't her fault if someone did not bring in their records and that we were only seeking the bank statements and financial records for the school so we could review them. However, we now also needed to know why the coach had not brought the sports account records to the school as requested.

We asked her to call the coach and tell him that the auditors were at the school and wanted him to bring the bank statements and financial records to the school that morning. We left her to make the call and went into a conference room to review the records that she had organized for us.

About 45 minutes later, the administrative employee came into the conference room and said that the coach was in the lobby with a box of records. We went to meet the coach and introduced ourselves. He looked very nervous. We then asked the coach to join us in the conference room. We told him we were conducting a review of the school's finances and as such we needed all of the school's bank statements. He still looked nervous.

Rather than diving right into things, I decided to take a different approach and see if his nervousness continued or diminished as we spoke. I asked him to tell us about the sports programs at the school. He described the various sports programs and teams and his family's involvement. He said that he and his wife had attended the school when they were younger, and now their children attended. During the conversation, his nervousness did not diminish. I asked him how the finances worked for the sports programs, and he told us about the fees and the nature of the program's expenses, like uniforms, field rental costs, and referee fees. Everything he said appeared straightforward and consistent, but he remained anxious.

We asked him if he'd brought all of the bank statements, paid invoices, and deposit records for the program, and he said that he had. When we asked him why he maintained the records at his house rather than the school, he said it had always been that way, and it was easier to keep everything together at his house. He said no one had ever asked him for the records in the past. We asked him why he hadn't brought them this morning as requested, and he said that he wanted to be able to explain them to the auditors when they reviewed them. His agitation grew.

We thanked him for bringing in the records and told him that we would go through them, along with all of the other accounts, and would circle back with him if we had any questions. As we finished our conversation, we asked him one final question: When we went through the financial records for the sports program, would we find anything that could be a potential issue regarding the finances and how they were handled?

He said that that was what he wanted to talk to the auditors about. He was now the most nervous he had been since we began talking. We asked him if he would like to tell us why he was so nervous. He said that when we went through the bank account, we would see expenses unrelated to the sports programs. We asked him to describe these types of expenses, and he said he wasn't sure if he should be talking with us. We told him that we understood and that we would get to the truth one way or the other once we reviewed the records. We also already knew about the credit card. We told him we weren't meeting with him to judge him, but rather we just wanted to get his side of the story about the school's sports program funds.

When he heard that, his face relaxed a bit, and he said that the check payments and credit-card charges were for personal and family expenses rather than school-related expenditures. We asked him to provide some detail about these expenses and spent the next hour or so going month by month through the bank statements, having him identify the personal expenses he'd paid with the school's sports funds. He also detailed how not all of the sports fees collected had been deposited, because he and his family had needed the funds at times to pay their mortgage or other expenses. Then he took us through the monthly credit-card statements, which revealed that the credit-card activity had nothing to do with the sports programs.

After reviewing all of the records, we thanked him for meeting with us. We told him he could have gone another way, by discarding all the records and declining to speak with us, but by being forthcoming, at least it was now all out on the table and we could work with the school, counsel, and him to resolve the issue of his misuse of school's funds. He looked much less stressed and nervous as we ended the meeting. ▦

At the outset of this matter, we'd had no idea there was a problem with the school's sports funds. We knew there had been an issue with the finance manager and with tuition and fees not being receipted and deposited into the school's bank accounts. However, we had no idea there was a completely separate issue with the sports program's finances. By listening respectfully to the administrative employee's story – and then treating the coach the same way – we were able to uncover a completely separate problem that was easier to quantify than the original issue.

ROLLERCOASTER

During a fraud engagement, individuals may become frustrated, angry, or depressed. They may break down and start crying during parts of their story and then turn angry during others. It is prudent to prepare for mood changes and expect a rollercoaster ride of emotions. Throughout it all, actively listen to clients and allow them time to regain their composure as needed. The impact of being a victim of fraud, or being accused of fraud, is very personal and the individual will likely be under a significant amount of stress. Their emotional state may be very unstable, and they may feel violated, especially if trusted family members or friends are involved in the matter, which is often the case.

It is important to note that while I discuss the victim's perspective in this book, these points are equally valid when the fraud examiner meets with other individuals involved in the matter. Regardless of the individual's role in the matter, everyone is entitled to the same genuine, objective, nonjudgmental, and respectful approach, and they are entitled to tell their story. Remember, there are three versions of every story, and the fraud examiner's goal is to determine the most important one, the only version that matters: the truth.

The role of the fraud examiner is to determine what happened, to the extent possible, given the limitations that arise in every case. Limitations often include missing information, lost or deleted files, and lack of access to key individuals involved in the matter. It is not the role of the fraud examiner to determine guilt or innocence. That determination is the sole responsibility of the trier of fact – the judge or the jury. Thus, to the extent practical, even in the most difficult matters the fraud examiner needs to set aside casting judgment and instead focus on obtaining the facts, which at times is easier said than done.

However, in determining the facts, it is also important to recognize that fraud examiners are only human, and some matters involve very difficult details, especially when children and physical abuse are involved. I discuss strategies for the fraud examiner dealing with their own emotions later in the book.

Before we continue this journal of client emotions, I think a brief discussion regarding feelings versus emotions is warranted. Merriam-Webster defines *feelings* as "one of the basic physical senses of which the skin contains the chief end organs and of which the sensations of touch and temperature are characteristic."[1] Included in the definition is "an emotional state or reaction."[2]

Merriam-Webster defines *emotions* as "a conscious mental reaction (such as anger or fear) subjectively experienced as strong feeling, usually directed toward a specific object and typically accompanied by physiological and behavioral changes in the body, a state of feeling."[3] While one definition appears to address to physical conditions while the other relates to nonphysical reactions, the terms have a relationship, as each word is used within the definition of the other. Throughout the rest of my book, I will refer to feelings and emotions simply as emotions.

In the next chapter, I advocate for an approach where the fraud examiner anticipates client emotions and chooses to address them rather than ignore them.

END NOTES

1. "Feeling," *Merriam-Webster Dictionary*, accessed January 11, 2021, https://www.merriam-webster.com/dictionary/feelings.
2. Ibid.
3. "Emotion," *Merriam-Webster Dictionary*, accessed January 11, 2021, https://www.merriam-webster.com/dictionary/emotion.

CHAPTER TWO

Choose to Address Client Emotions

EXPECT CLIENT EMOTIONS

Client matters typically start with a phone call, email, or other form of communication requesting fraud-related services. At my firm, we almost always receive a phone call, an email, or a voice message requesting that we call a prospective client. During that initial call, my staff and I try to get an idea of what the matter involves, along with the names of the parties involved. We perform a procedure we call "triage," where we complete an intake form to ensure we've captured the party names, attorney names (if attorneys are involved at that point), a short description of the matter, and the issues requiring our services. We then perform a conflict search to ensure that we can be objective and free of any conflicts of interest, such as a relationship to the issues or parties in the matter.

Our forms are saved in a three-ring binder. If we end up performing services in the case, we move the form into the matter folder. If we don't end up having an initial meeting or are not retained, we save the forms within the original binder. Often, we receive subsequent calls about a potential matter that is surprisingly familiar to us. We then stop the call and scan through our forms, quite often finding that we have received a previous call about the same matter. Unless the caller is the same person who originally called us, we have to inform the new caller that we've received a prior call in which details of the case were shared with us, and for that reason, we have to decline involvement the matter, as a conflict of interest likely exists.

During the initial call, while we are obtaining a short version of the matter, we also try to gain an understanding of the potential client's emotional state. If the caller has not provided us with details about the other parties and their emotional states (as they often do, unsolicited), we ask about those as part of our triage process. Knowing that every matter has emotional issues, we look for certain key emotions, such as anger and hostility, especially in the parties on the opposing side of the matter. First and foremost, our concern is our safety, and knowing whether one or more parties has anger issues is critical to our well-being. It's also helpful for us to know when a party with anger issues possesses a weapons permit or hunting interests (these circumstances cause the hairs on our neck to stand up).

In many cases, the caller is an attorney representing a client. In some other cases, the individuals who call our office represent an organization or are pursuing a personal matter. In those cases, part of our triage process involves instructing the individual to obtain counsel, since my firm's policy is that our services can only be retained through counsel. We do this to establish attorney–client privilege under the attorney work-product doctrine. We also ask that clients instruct their attorney to call us, once the attorney has been retained, so we can discuss the potential matter and solicit more details.

When the client's attorney calls, they often describe their client's emotional state. If for some reason they don't, we ask them about emotional states as part of our triage process. When the client has a longstanding relationship with the attorney, we often receive a lot of background detail about the client and their emotional state. However, if the attorney is new to the client, we often are limited to comparing initial notes and impressions and must wait for the initial meeting to gather more detail.

While obtaining a brief summary of the matter, a fraud examiner should already be thinking about the types of emotions involved in the potential matter – not just the client's emotions, but the emotions of other parties involved as well. A fraud examiner can often predict the likely emotions to be encountered based on the limited facts provided, as well as how long the potential matter has been going on. The duration of the matter up to that point is often a good predictor of the emotional state of the parties.

If the potential matter has just been discovered or initiated, we often encounter denial or anger. If the matter has been pending for months or even years, the range of potential emotions can be much greater. As I discuss later in the book, individuals involved in financial matters requiring a fraud examiner often experience similar emotional states to people going through the grieving process (e.g., denial, anger, bargaining, depression, and acceptance). Depending on the timeline of the matter, the fraud examiner may be able to estimate the parties' emotional states. (I choose the word "estimate" rather than "predict," as I have sometimes been surprised to see the client's actual emotional state when we meet.)

Where practical, the fraud examiner should begin every new matter with an initial in-person meeting. If the potential client cannot meet in person, the examiner should set up a virtual call. It's important for the fraud examiner to see the potential client, to visually assess them while listening to them talk. In these meetings, an experienced fraud examiner can gain a sense of the client's emotional state and size up whether they want to work with them. The same holds true in meeting an attorney. My firm has walked away from many great cases because we didn't want to work with a client or their attorney based on an impression we picked up on during the meeting.

In a few rare instances, my firm has lost a referral source for declining our involvement in a potential matter, but experience has shown me that I need to trust my instincts. When my sixth sense tells me something isn't right about an individual or a matter, I know I need to walk away. In some cases, I need to run. That turned out to be the case in the following story, where my instincts alerted me to something "not right" in the client's story.

I had scheduled a meeting with an attorney I'd worked with on past cases, regarding a matter where employees were stealing funds from an organization. As I regularly do, I brought someone from my office with me so the two of us could listen to the potential matter, assess emotional states, ask questions, and take notes. Often, the person I bring is the person who will work on the matter with me, so they can hear things firsthand right from the inception.

When we arrived, we met the attorney and several individuals who were sitting at a conference table. As the attorney introduced us to his clients, each expressed how excited they were to meet us and to gain our help in resolving their matter.

After the introductions, one of the individuals sitting at the head of the table identified himself as the executive director. He started talking about the organization, what it did, the locations that it had, the systems that it used . . . all to provide us background on the issues he was about to describe. He identified one particular location where he and the others in the meeting believed employees had been diverting funds. The primary people running the location were all related to each other: a husband and wife, their children, and other relatives. The executive director described the system that was used at the location, along with the system's known vulnerabilities.

Members of the parent organization had analyzed the activity of the location based on system reports for the past several years and found significant issues. Sales volume was too low and appeared to be manipulated – and although this location was one of their busiest, the sales volume and trends made no sense when compared to their other locations, which used the same systems. The executive director said that he and the others in the meeting were very frustrated with the individuals at that location and wanted to press further based on the initial analyses, but that they thought it would be more prudent to bring in an objective, neutral consultant, such as a fraud examiner, to further analyze the location's activity.

Listening to his story and looking at the very detailed analyses and spreadsheets they'd prepared, something just didn't feel right to me. I couldn't understand why, with the level of detail collected and analyzed, they didn't just go to law enforcement with their work and ask them to initiate a criminal investigation. I asked the group that very question. They responded that they wanted to be more thorough and prudent by getting an independent assessment. Their responses didn't make sense to me. Something seemed wrong.

The meeting continued, with the executive director telling us he had given his notice and would only be with the organization for another two weeks. I found that information troubling as well. I wondered what was really happening at the meeting and why this organization wanted to bring in outside fraud examiners when they had done much of the analysis themselves and at the time their executive director was leaving.

I asked them to describe the individuals who worked at the location in question. The executive director said the family was very close and controlled everything that happened at the location. He said that non-family members had worked there in the past, but whenever they did not go along with what the family wanted, they were fired. Turnover among non-family members was high, higher than at any other location. The executive director said he believed that the family was skimming cash from the daily sales and then concealing the thefts in the system, which would account for the sales and trends being so different from the other locations. The executive director said that the family members were not nice people and controlled all hours of operations by having at least one family member on hand at all times to watch over things. The family members had been very hostile toward other workers and had developed a sense of independence from the corporate office. Although the family had received requests for information as well as access to their systems, to date they had provided neither.

I sensed that the executive director and the others feared these individuals, something that made me very uncomfortable.

While my instinct was to decline our involvement, I first asked to know more about the family. The executive director said that the father, the patriarch of the operation, was also known as the unofficial "king" of his neighborhood, in one of the poorer areas of the city known for gang-related activity and violence. I wondered to myself whether, had I not asked this question, the group would have kept that tidbit of information from us – a tidbit that formed a critical element relating to our safety if we were to get involved in the matter. I wondered what else the group had left out – and what their real motive was for our involvement.

Once the group finished talking, they asked me for my thoughts on how to proceed with their matter. I think they were shocked by my reaction and what I said next. I will never forget how their moods changed in response.

I told them that, given the background and history of the individuals working at the location, the lack of cooperation and access to information, and especially the patriarch's unofficial title of "king" of a rather violent neighborhood, that they were crazy for not getting law enforcement involved, if for no other reason than to minimize the safety issues for everyone involved. The fact that they possessed a detailed analysis showing some type of theft occurring but were reluctant to get law enforcement involved did not sit right with me. Something seemed wrong with this potential matter and what they were telling us (or more importantly, what they were not telling us).

I asked them what they thought would happen if they were correct and the family was stealing daily proceeds from the organization. What would happen when that cash flow suddenly stopped? I told them I was not going to get involved unless the group also involved law enforcement. They told me that involving the police was not an option at that time.

Well, at that point, the meeting took a significant turn. After saying they didn't understand why we wouldn't get involved in the matter, they began to get angry. They started asking pointed questions about why we would not take on this matter. As the mood in the room shifted, I knew I had made the right decision. My sixth sense had been telling me something was wrong, and it was. We ended the meeting and left before the discussion went any further.

As of this writing, their attorney – who had used our services on several matters prior to this meeting – has never called us again, nor has he been receptive to subsequent communication from us. Worse, when we referred a client to him and the client ended up using his firm, the attorney didn't even bother to thank us for the referral. Apparently, because of my declining involvement in his matter, he chose to no longer have any business dealings with me or my firm. It happens. ▪

When we returned to the office we conducted some research into the entity and individuals, and also subsequently monitored the matter through news stories. It turned out that our sixth sense was accurate, picking up on the red flags during the meeting – things like the group's holding back on details and their reluctance to involve law enforcement. We learned more about the targets of our investigation, who were known to law enforcement and ran some of the unsavory areas of the city. We also learned that a fabled attempt to install clandestine surveillance equipment failed when some of the targeted individuals randomly happened upon the men installing the cameras, which eliminated any element of surprise. All in all, we decided we had made the right decision in walking away from that matter.

 ## ADDRESS CLIENT EMOTIONS

Once we decide a potential matter is one we want to get involved in, we discuss our expectations with the client at the first meeting. I encourage every fraud examiner to establish ground rules with new clients at the inception of a new matter (a process I explore in more detail later in the book). In the initial meeting, we discuss how our firm typically communicates with clients and their attorneys, and we provide our contact information, including email addresses. We tell them that my firm's hours of operations are weekdays from 8 a.m. to 5 p.m. and that we monitor both email and voicemail throughout the day and evening. We also tell them that they can expect a response from someone in our firm within a day of leaving a message, although it is almost always much, much sooner. However, we do not constantly check emails and voice messages, as that can be distracting when working on other client matters. Therefore, we periodically review messages throughout the day and then provide responses. We also let clients know that, unlike many of the world's smartphone users, we do not receive emails on our phones, so there will be a delay between the time they send an email and the time they receive a response.

Fraud examiners should ensure that all the communications on a matter comply with counsel's expectations to best ensure the attorney–client privilege throughout the duration of the matter. In most cases, the attorney will request to be included on all communications, and you should expect to include the attorney on all communications even when the client fails to do so.

If a client communicates with us without including their attorney on the exchange, our practice is to add the attorney back onto our responses and add a reminder to the client to be sure to include the attorney on all future communications. Although many clients will comply with your reminder, many will not – for a variety of reasons, including trying to minimize the attorney's billable time on the matter. Regardless, we add the attorney and the reminder every time.

In some cases, a client will become angry after you add the attorney back on to the communication and will call or send you a heated email. Once they vent, remind them that the attorney–client privilege is there to protect them and prevent any unwanted disclosure of information about their matter. My experience has been that the client will understand this explanation, and the issue will go away – at least until the next time their attorney is added back onto a communication. Remember: Your persistence is more important than their reasoning for not wanting to include their attorney on communications.

In our first meeting, we also discuss the different emotions the client will likely encounter while their matter is pending resolution. We tell them they will probably become frustrated – if they are not already – due to the time it takes to resolve financial matters. We tell them that they may get angry at times, possibly because of delays or costs or because of an unfavorable decision or limitation in their case. We tell them that we will be patient and responsive and will give them the best information available each time they reach out to us. However, they can expect at times that we may not have much information with which to update them.

We try to end each initial meeting by setting the client's expectations at a realistic level. By doing so, we create a way to bring the client back to reality when they have bad days during the pendency of their matter – and they *will* have bad days.

As cynical as this may sound, after 31 years of experience in this field, I tell clients to set their expectations at "disappointed." I tell them that, in the end, if they are disappointed by the ultimate outcome of their matter, then their initial expectations have been met. If the outcome or results exceed their expectation of disappointment, then they will have done better than most.

I learned this strategy (which I like to call "Sales 101") through manager training I received working at a public accounting firm. The training we received was based on sales training used by car dealers with their sales staff. There, I learned that the recipe for satisfied customers was to meet or beat customer expectations every time. The only way to accomplish this regularly was to set customer expectations at a realistic level. Sadly, I have found that most fraud cases result in disappointment at some level, whether it relates to the amount recovered, the consequences and accountability (or lack thereof) for the perpetrator, or the court's decision against the client's position.

The fraud examiner, also, must set his or her sights on a likely disappointing outcome, since it's difficult to predict how cases will play out in a court of law. In such cases, it's difficult not to absorb some of the client's emotions – as is illustrated in the following story.

We were retained to work with counsel to investigate a fiduciary's actions within an estate and a conservatorship. A fiduciary is someone who is put into a position of trust over someone else's assets and affairs. The beneficiaries of an estate had retained counsel and claimed that the fiduciary, who was also an attorney managing the estate's financial affairs, was stealing from the estate and conservatorship. The estate in question belonged to a husband and wife who never had any children. The beneficiaries to the estate, all relatives, lived out of state. The court named the attorney as the woman's conservator, which created the fiduciary position.

The woman had contacted her relatives and, during their discussions, indicated that she thought the attorney was stealing from her. The family was angry at the news but lacked local resources to oversee the attorney's activities. The woman's relatives contacted local counsel, who in turn retained our services. One of the aspects of this case involved the woman's physical estate, upon which there was a primary residence and a guest house. During the period that the attorney was the fiduciary, long before our involvement, one of the woman's nephews had started looking into the finances handled by the attorney. The more the nephew investigated, the more he discovered things that made no sense. The nephew visited the house and saw how the attorney and his wife controlled nearly every aspect of his aunt's life. It appeared to him that his aunt was solely dependent on the attorney and his wife and lacked the freedom to do anything for herself, including going to the market and the bank. The more the nephew learned what was happening, the more he grew suspicious.

Those involved in this case believe that at some point the attorney became aware of the nephew's observations and decided to meet with the nephew. To this day, neither the attorney nor the nephew will confirm the meeting or discuss what transpired during it, but afterwards, the attorney transferred the house at the back of the estate into the nephew's name. Once the house was transferred, the nephew moved in and made the house his primary residence. After the transfer, the nephew never gave us any further details, nor did he cooperate with the investigation.

Laws require that fiduciaries, such as conservators, obtain the court's permission prior to selling or transferring significant assets, such as real estate. In this case, the attorney neither requested nor provided such permission. This was a significant factor in the beneficiaries seeking to have the house transfer reversed and the house placed back into the estate.

The land record reflected a transfer form signed by the aunt, with an "X" as her signature. Counsel for the beneficiaries requested copies of the woman's medical records and also interviewed in-home care staff who were present during the period when the transfer took place. The medical records showed that the woman suffered from dementia and other significant health issues and had been primarily bedridden at the time of the transfer. The caregivers stated that the woman would not have known what she was signing at the time of the transfer. These additional factors gave the beneficiaries hope of recovering the house back into the estate.

The fiduciary attorney had stated through his counsel that the aunt told him she wanted her nephew to have the house and told the attorney to transfer the house into the nephew's name. The attorney said he had witnessed the woman sign the transfer form and that she had signed her name with an "X," as she commonly did around that time period.

We discovered no other documents signed by the aunt, let alone any signed with an "X," since the attorney had signed nearly all transactions using his name and the phrase "as her conservator." This was yet another significant piece of information.

One particular beneficiary, angry that the attorney had exploited the woman, brought an action in court to recover the house. Given the information surrounding the transfer, it appeared a court would see what happened, determine it was a fraudulent transfer, and revert the house back to the estate.

Months passed after the lawsuit was initiated, and the beneficiaries grew more and more frustrated at the delay caused by the process, especially knowing that the nephew lived at the house day in and day out without any repercussions.

Finally, the court date arrived. We met at the courthouse and discussed the trial strategy with counsel in the hallway. The beneficiary's attorney brought witnesses and evidence to show the judge what had happened with the transfer. Things seemed to be going well for the beneficiary's case. Next, opposing counsel put the nephew on the witness stand. The nephew told the court about how much his aunt wanted him to have the house and live on the property. He described his life before he moved into the house and noted how his life had significantly improved after receiving it.

Although we thought his story was irrelevant, opposing counsel's strategy was to have the judge hear it. The case ended with final arguments, and we then waited for a decision.

There is no other way to describe our reactions to the decision than "blown away." Even though the law was in the beneficiary's favor, as were the medical records and testimony of the caregivers, the judge ruled to allow the nephew to keep the house. I observed the shell-shocked and disbelieving look on the beneficiary's face, and I knew it would transition from disbelief to anger, so I quickly escorted him out of court and to his car. As we walked, he asked me what had just happened. I told him I had no idea. We waited by our cars for his attorney, and when the attorney arrived, I asked him to explain the ruling. The law had been on our side, the facts had been on our side, and the witnesses had been on our side. I said it appeared pretty clear to me that what the attorney had done constituted buying off the nephew to stop him from looking into his aunt's financial affairs. The beneficiary asked his attorney how the judge could rule in favor of the nephew keeping the house.

The attorney responded: "The judge made an emotional decision today, not a legal one."

I wondered, "What does that even mean? That judges can disregard the laws and make 'emotional' decisions?" I asked the attorney how this was possible.

The attorney replied, "It happens sometimes."

In the meantime, the beneficiary was growing more and more angry. He verbalized his anger, citing the amount of time and money that he had spent getting to today's trial date, only for the judge to make an emotional decision. Suffice to say, he was upset. I calmed him down enough for him to drive and waited until he and his attorney had left in their cars.

I too was shell-shocked and angry at what had just happened. It had shattered my belief that judges who hold the highest position within the legal system would reach emotional decisions.

The good news in this matter: Subsequent actions taken by the beneficiaries resulted in the recovery of the house from the nephew as well as the recovery of $4.8 million in diverted funds. However, this recovery did not take place until the beneficiaries had spent even more money and the fiduciary attorney had been prosecuted and convicted. ▪

This case illustrates how a fraud examiner can experience emotions similar to those of his clients while working on an engagement. While it's important to not become too emotionally involved in client cases, I know that, once retained, I become very intimate with the details of a case, often knowing them better than anyone else. I also know (or at least choose to continue to believe) that if everything works as it is supposed to, then the system will prevail in favor of the truth, and the right decision or outcome will be achieved. Sadly, there is no guaranteed outcome when it comes to court and legal proceedings, even with the best evidence to support a client's position. Fraud examiners are human, and it's hard not to feel the same emotional reactions as clients – especially when you've invested so much effort into determining what actually happened – only to have the legal process reach a decision that is contrary to the evidence. Unfortunately, that does happen sometimes.

To make matters worse, after receiving an unfavorable decision or outcome, we must close the file and send the client a final invoice. We know we are just concluding our involvement and that the client expects to receive a final invoice, but we also know how the client may react when they receive it (along with their attorney's bill). It's only human for the client to be not only angry at losing a case but also angry at having to send additional funds to pay for outstanding costs. In some cases, you will receive full payment from the client, but in others you can expect to do some level of bargaining and compromise in order to get the final payment.

In the next chapter, we discuss complicating factors when it comes to dealing with client emotions.

CHAPTER THREE

Complicating Factors

THE *CSI* EFFECT

Many factors influence client emotions, and nearly all of them are beyond the fraud examiner's control. Most often these factors impact when and how the client's matter will be resolved, which in turn affects their emotional state at any given time. A challenge fraud examiners face is that clients' emotional states can and will change quite frequently. Their emotions alter given what is happening (or not happening) in their case, along with events in all the other aspects of their lives, nearly all of which the fraud examiner will not be aware of when first taking on the case.

In the past 15 years or so, television shows like *Law & Order*, *CSI: Crime Scene Investigation*, *NCIS*, *Criminal Minds*, and others have directly influenced clients' expectations, and in turn clients' emotions. Many viewers have gravitated toward these shows, mesmerized by Hollywood's ability to solve crimes within an hour-long format, using blood samples, tiny morsels of physical evidence, computer files, trace DNA samples, and voice and facial recognition. Viewers watch as investigators use state-of-the-art technology to scan images, re-create complete vehicle details based on faint tire marks, form connections between fragments of evidence, establish timelines based on data that simply does not exist in real life, and obtain accurate responses from other agencies and institutions within minutes of their request. The reality is that while some of these feats are possible, things move much more slowly and with far less accuracy in real life.

The fraud examiner encounters a challenge when their client applies what they've seen on television to their own case and expects the same swift resolution for their own matter. I call this tendency "the *CSI* effect." The problem is that much of what the client has seen on those shows is inaccurate, and to the extent that they are reflective of reality, the solutions on TV are often not readily available to fraud examiners outside of governmental agencies (and even then, only in certain cases).

For example, many clients believe that there is a database, comprised of every bank and investment account in existence, held at every bank, credit union, and brokerage house in the country. These same clients believe that a query made to the database will reveal every financial account belonging to an individual, even those that were closed many years ago. A second query will produce all of the bank statements, canceled check images, and other records relating to each and every account. Unfortunately, the reality is that no such database exists.

On television, investigators use video footage to determine who perpetrated a crime. Clients expect the same results when video cameras are in use at places relating to their case. The reality is that even if footage exists (and often it does not), it can be grainy and difficult to view with any degree of clarity. In many cases in which footage was initially taken, too much time has passed and the footage is no longer available. On television, investigators somehow obtain access to footage, even extremely old images, and use technology in their labs to clarify details that ultimately lead them to the suspect. While I wouldn't state with certainty that such technology does not exist – because I'm sure it does at some level – the reality is that most fraud examiners do not have access to this type of technology.

As I discussed earlier, the fraud examiner has an opportunity at the initial meeting to address client expectations and set them at a realistic level, thus minimizing client upset down the road. We often ask the client if they watch any of these types of television shows, and if so, if they have any expectations about how a fraud examiner can conduct procedures and work toward resolving a matter. Based on their responses, we provide them with a realistic picture of what we can do based on the information, systems, tools, and procedures available to us. We also discuss the limitations fraud examiners often encounter, such as whether individuals are available, accessible, and cooperative enough to interview, and whether sufficient records and information have been located and are available for our review. We tell the client that creating a complete and accurate picture of a matter is a rare occurrence, so we work within the constraints of our limitations and provide the best picture possible based on the information and individuals available to us. In some instances, we aren't able to determine what happened due to significant limitations. Unfortunately, these kinds of roadblocks do occur, especially because individuals committing fraud and other wrongdoing tend to discard or destroy evidence of their activities. We can also be thwarted in our efforts when too much time has transpired and records are no longer available to review.

If you discuss these issues with the client in advance and set their expectations at an appropriate level (somewhere around "disappointed"), you're far more likely to successfully manage their emotions.

What does all this mean? The fraud examiner should be prepared for their client to be disappointed. The fraud examination field, much like any other type of field, is plagued by limitations. The client will often be desperate and will attend the meeting with high hopes that the fraud examiner, coupled with cutting-edge CSI technology, will successfully (almost magically) solve their case by finding the key pieces to the puzzle. However, by the end of the meeting, the client will learn the realities of what can and cannot be done, which often results in bursting their bubble. That certainly was the case in the following engagement involving family members who were desperate to have a fraud examiner locate a significant amount of missing money.

We attended a meeting with a potential client and his attorney regarding a theft matter after the death of the client's uncle. After introductions, I asked the potential client to explain what had happened and why he thought he needed a fraud examiner. The gentleman provided us with the following story.

His uncle had lived alone in another state, had never married, and had no children. About six months earlier, his uncle had passed away. Upon learning of his death, the client drove to his uncle's house to meet other family members. Upon their arrival, they went into the basement to locate and secure a box of cash that the uncle was known to have kept. After searching the last-known location, as well as the rest of the house, the client and his relatives determined that the box of cash was gone. Several family members had been familiar with the uncle's box of cash, since the uncle had showed it to many of them at various times.

The client described the box in great detail and estimated that it contained more than $500,000. He remembered when his uncle had reached a half-million dollars, because his uncle was proud of his savings and made a big deal about it at the time. The only explanation for the box of cash being missing was that someone who knew about the box had gone to the house prior to the client's arrival and taken it.

The uncle had a will that named the client as a beneficiary of his estate. The client said he was to receive an equal share of the estate, along with three other family members. He estimated that he would have received at least $125,000 had the cash not been stolen. He'd reported the theft to the police, but they'd told him there was little they could do since there were no cameras or other surveillance showing who had been at the house. The police told the client the box of cash could be anywhere and had perhaps even been stolen before his uncle's death.

Once the client finished with his story, he asked us what we could do to help resolve the matter. I could sense the desperation in his face and voice. Unfortunately, I had to tell him that there was really nothing a fraud examiner could do to determine who took the box of cash without some type of lead as to who may have gone to the house before the other relatives. I then watched as his face lit up. He was anxious to add more details to his story.

He and his family believed that a cousin and her son had gone to the house as soon as they heard about his uncle's passing and had taken the box for themselves. Everyone in the family believed that these relatives had made two trips: their initial one to steal the box of cash, and a second one with the other family members. I asked the client why he and his family thought the cousin and her son were the thieves. He said the cousin had never had much money and her adult son lived with her. They had a small, ordinary house and older cars. However, a few months after his uncle passed away, they were both driving new cars, the son had moved into his own house, and the loan on his cousin's house had been paid off. Once he and his family members saw these changes, they knew who had taken the uncle's money, since the cousin and her son had no other known sources of significant funds.

Once again, the client stopped, looking to us to bring the cousin and her son to justice for stealing his uncle's cash.

He and his family were angry with his cousin and her son for stealing the funds and spending the inheritance on themselves. The client was desperate because he had tried so many avenues to hold them accountable and recover any remaining funds, all to no avail. He said he was becoming very depressed over the matter and that we were his last hope. He said $100,000 would make a significant difference in his life, especially since he'd recently lost his job. He was the sole provider for his family, and the inheritance would make a significant improvement in his family's lifestyle. He wouldn't even be at this meeting if it weren't for his cousin and her son stealing the funds. Angry and upset, he pleaded with us, saying that there must be a way a fraud examiner could determine what had happened to the box of cash.

I told him that the reality of the matter was that if his family's guess was accurate and the cousin and her son had stolen the cash and spent it, they had likely left a paper trail of their spending through purchasing cars and a house and paying off a mortgage. I told him the road to resolving the allegation would have to start through a legal process, not a fraud examination. He would have to use his attorney to file a suit against the cousin and her son, alleging theft, which would then provide his attorney with a means to subpoena the cousin and her son's financial records. The attorney's ability to take depositions and ask questions under oath might allow him to determine the truth about the source of their recent funds. However, the client would first have to bring a formal allegation against his cousin and her son. The client's attorney agreed.

I told the client that if he decided to go down that path and his efforts resulted in access to the cousin and her son's financial records, a fraud examiner could then help him review their financial records to determine the source of their funds. Until then, however, there was no productive role for a fraud examiner, since there were no financial records to examine beyond the land records he'd already obtained.

Over the course of our conversation, the gentleman's emotional state changed completely. He appeared to move from desperate to hopeful. Near the end of the meeting, he said he finally had an optimistic outlook because he had a potential path toward determining what happened. He knew the process could reveal that the cousin and her son did not in fact steal the box of cash – or worse, that they might have done such a good job of hiding the stolen cash that their records would not reflect the theft. However, he was finally hopeful that he had a means of proving the suspected theft.

The client thanked us for the meeting, and we never heard from him or his attorney again. We will never know if he and his family sued the cousin and her son, or whether his matter was ever resolved. The only thing we know for sure is that we provided him and his family members with hope. ▪

Managing a client's expectations will greatly assist you when it comes to predicting and responding to their emotions. In many fraud cases, financial records, tax returns, and bank statements are available for review. Even if they are incomplete, these limited records provide the fraud examiner with a starting point that often leads to identifying additional financial records that need to be requested. In some instances, the financial records can be reproduced – for instance, bank statements from a financial institution or tax return transcripts from the federal or state taxing authorities. However, there are limitations even to these sources of information, such as how far back records are maintained. In other instances, there simply is little to nothing for the fraud examiner to work with, and the trail to additional records and information runs cold. It's important to be honest with clients about these limitations, even if it involves deflating their expectations.

 ## FAMILY AND "LIKE FAMILY" RELATIONSHIPS

Another complicating factor influencing client emotions is the client's relationship with other parties involved in the matter. These relationships can be formal, such as family connections, or less formal, such as bonds with coworkers or friends. Further complicating matters is the nature and length of each relationship.

Especially when family members are involved, client emotions can run deep, and their feelings may be intertwined with events that occurred a long, long time ago – in some cases all the way back to childhood. For reasons usually unknown to the fraud examiner, the client chooses the fraud matter as a forum to address those lingering past issues. When crossed by another family member, a client may feel violated, hurt, angry, or even hostile – and nothing creates more bad feelings than one family member stealing from another.

Family issues often prevent the client from making reasonable decisions, since the client is often distracted by ancillary concerns such as needing to right a wrong, seeking parental validation, or simply winning based on principle. For example, a sibling who feels that another sibling received more love or preferential treatment from a parent will no doubt find these emotions triggered when these family members are involved in a fraud investigation. The fraud examiner should expect that these issues will come out during a matter.

I have experienced many fraud matters involving families: parents against children, children against parents, and siblings against siblings. In these cases, emotions ran very high, and often the fighting, yelling, screaming, and crying we witnessed had nothing to do with the specific aspects of the fraud matter. As a fraud examiner witnessing these interactions, you will likely be unaware of the underlying issues. Each family member likely has a suitcase of past issues they are bringing with them and will use the present case as an opportunity to air and resolve their outstanding family issues.

From an outsider's perspective, I have found it very sad to see the impact these cases have on family dynamics and the toll they take on family members. Often, family members stop speaking to one another, and in some cases, they cannot even occupy the same room without becoming violent. I've often sat in these meetings and wondered what life was like for the family before all of the current issues began. Resentment is a powerful and common emotion that is often associated with family disputes. Cases involving family members can result in hostility, anger, tears, and depression.

As a fraud examiner, remember that your personal safety is paramount, as is your staff's well-being. Taking time to consider things like where to meet someone, who should be present, and where you sit during a meeting are all important in minimizing safety issues while conducting fraud examinations, especially highly emotional ones.

In some cases the fraud examiner may be able to identify safety risks and predict things that could go wrong while working on a fraud matter, such as when opposing parties meet for the first time after a fraud investigation has been initiated, as was the case with the following matter.

We worked on a matter where one sibling was the primary caregiver for her mother, while the other siblings were less involved. At the inception of this arrangement, everything seemed to be working for everyone. The siblings would come over to their sister's house to visit with their mother, and everyone had a good time. Mom was receiving quality care as well as companionship from the sister. However, as often happens, over time things started to change at the sister's house. She completed renovations on her house, and a new car sat in her driveway. The siblings started asking their sister where she was getting the funds for these things, and the sister started shutting down communication and shutting her siblings out of their mother's life. Soon, visits came to a halt because the sister would claim that their mother was not going to be home or that their mother was not feeling well. Over time, the other siblings lost all access to their mother and to her financial information. The siblings continually tried to gain access to their mother, to no avail, and so they eventually sought legal assistance. Weeks became months, and months dragged out into over a year. The siblings were frustrated, angry, and desperate to see their mother. They wanted to know that she was being properly cared for, but still they gained no access.

Finally, the siblings received word that their mother had passed away. One can only imagine the world of emotions the siblings experienced after learning that their mother, whom they had not seen in a long time and had not had opportunity to say goodbye to, had died. An experienced fraud examiner should recognize that, although a court could hold the sister accountable for her handling of her mother's financial affairs, there was nothing the court could do to repair the emotional damage caused by the sister's actions.

As if this story was not bad enough, more distressing information about the mother's care came out as part of the investigation and court process. Another family member who had access to the sister's house during the period the siblings were locked out reported that the sister had required her mother to spend all of her time in a windowless basement, which she was barred from leaving. The sister threatened to place the mother in a nursing home if she ever tried to leave the basement or tell anyone about her living conditions. The witness said the mother lived in fear every day, was malnourished, and lacked quality medical care.

We were able to confirm some of the witness's details through the mother's financial records. The sister was using the mother's assets and monthly income to bolster her own family's lifestyle and had squandered her mother's life savings. Knowing that their mother had in essence been held prisoner in their sister's house right up until her death, while their sister spent all of their mother's funds on herself and her family, the siblings were pushed over the edge emotionally. No outcomes short of prison for their sister would be acceptable, and it was pointless to discuss any other potential resolution. ▪

I share this story as an example of how the fraud examiner needs to anticipate the emotions that will come into play during their involvement in a matter. A fraud examiner should attempt to understand how they would feel if placed in a similar situation to their clients. In the story I relayed above, it would be unrealistic to suppose that the siblings would be willing to compromise simply to settle their matter. They could not walk away from what their sister had done to their mother. My experiences in these matters have taught me that there is no way this type of case will ever settle, short of the siblings having their sister's head on a platter – and even then they will likely still want more consequences. A fraud examiner would be ill-prepared and foolish not to anticipate a high potential for violence when these siblings first meet in the same room as their sister after learning about the care and treatment of their mother.

Fraud examiners should anticipate violence, expect it, plan for it, and make arrangements for other resources – possibly the police – to be present in those kinds of meetings. Tensions will run high at any meeting and in every other instance the parties cross paths, until the case is resolved. The fraud examiner's planning should account for not only the time during meetings, but also each individual's time from when they leave their car to attend the meetings, as well as the time it takes the individuals to exit the meetings and head back to their cars. Client emotions don't get boxed up and stored before and after a meeting, to appear only during a meeting. The emotions are always present, and emotional interactions can occur whenever and wherever parties see each other. I have experienced many such encounters between parties in hallways and parking lots.

Some of my most memorable meetings that went poorly – fueled by emotions, anger, and hostility – involved family members, family finances, and the treatment of family members. However, relationships are not limited to families. Personal friendships and work relationships can become just as strong as family relationships, especially when the bonds have been in place for a long time. In many cases, an individual may be closer to their friends and coworkers than they are to their actual family. Most people spend as much time at their job as they do at home (and sometimes more so), and often friendships and coworker relationships last longer than family relationships.

As an example, let's look at how friendships may become more important than a marriage. A person may have had friendships that started long before they met their spouse. If the marriage fails, the friendships often continue, and thus the friendships last longer than the person's marriage. The following story illustrates how a friendship or coworker relationship can impact client emotions on the same scale as a family relationship.

Two best friends decided to leave their jobs and start a business together. They were excited at the opportunity to work day in and day out with each other. They formed an entity and decided to split things equally, and for the next several years everything worked as planned. Both individuals seemed very happy with their arrangement. But then things changed, as they often do. One partner was dealing with personal issues, and he started spending less time at the business. Perhaps one source of his distraction was the affair he was having with the business's bookkeeper. At any rate, the bookkeeping fell behind, the friend started spending even less time at the business, and the other owner was left behind to do everything.

As time went on, the friend left running the business grew more and more resentful – not just because his friend never did anything with the business yet continued to receive half of the profits, but also because he knew his friend's wife and family. What had started out as a fling with the bookkeeper had now taken a significant toll on his friend's marriage and children. As time rolled on, the owner running the business tried to talk sense into his friend, only to be brushed aside. Eventually, the owner made the decision to find a new bookkeeper, and then he changed the locks on the business. For a while nothing changed, since the friend never came to the business anyway. However, soon thereafter, the owner running the business adjusted the payouts, allocating proportionally more to himself for his work and less to his friend, who was never around. One day, the friend came to the business after hours, only to find he couldn't gain access to the building. He called his friend to find out why his income had been cut and why his key wouldn't open the doors. When his access and income continued to be reduced, he retained counsel to sue his best friend, feeling angry and betrayed by this turn of events. ▧

A fraud examiner has to imagine the potential client emotions that either individual might experience in a case like this, and recognize that each friend's emotions will be completely different based on their unique perspectives. Now, I will add one more twist to the story, because there are always twists in these cases.

At some point prior to the friend's learning he was locked out of the business, his wife learned of his affair and left him. She then filed for divorce and sole custody of their children. Now separated from her husband, she realized she needed to get a job to support herself and her family. She turned to the friend who was still running the business, and then started working at the company as the new bookkeeper. ▧

How would this new twist impact the client emotions on either side of the case? Resentment, betrayal, anger, and frustration are all very common in such instances.

The friend's ex-wife was now working for his best friend, in the very business he'd started with his friend, from which he was locked out and deprived of income due to his affair. Both friends raised allegations of financial improprieties, creating the need for a fraud examiner to conduct a complete and objective review of the business's financial affairs. ▧

You can't make these scenarios up – they really happen. (In case you were wondering, this was an actual case I witnessed while working for counsel representing the friend who'd continued to run the business. And no, a new relationship did not start between him and his friend's ex-wife, although his friend thought for sure that they were in fact in an intimate relationship.)

In another example, four women worked together for years in the billing department of a small medical practice. They kept pictures of their children and families on their desks, and the shortest coworking relationship that existed in the group spanned 18 years. They celebrated birthdays and holidays together, in and outside of work. They shared their family stories and attended weddings and funerals for each other's families. Suffice to say, they were close friends.

One day, one of the women was out sick, and another woman covered her duties, which included opening the mail and processing insurance checks. Looking for a deposit slip, she opened her coworker's desk and found a short stack of undeposited checks and an endorsement stamp different from the one used by the practice. The endorsement stamp was for a bank account in the practice's name, but at a financial institution for which the practice had no bank accounts. Puzzled by her findings, the woman brought the practice manager over to clear up her confusion. The practice manager had no idea why this employee would have an endorsement stamp or any undeposited checks in her desk and so alerted one of the doctor owners. The doctor and practice manager drove to the bank, only to learn that there was a bank account with activity in the name of the practice at that bank. It made no sense, and so they called their attorney for advice, as they wanted to be sure they didn't jump to any conclusions or create any exposure for the practice.

The woman whose endorsement stamp had been discovered had been a great employee and longstanding friend to the practice. The attorney called me, and based on the story he told me, I knew they had found evidence of wrongdoing. Within a very short period, I gained access to the bank statements and deposit details for the bank account the employee had opened. We determined she had been stealing for years, skimming insurance checks and depositing them into an account that she had opened and controlled. In total, she'd stolen over $250,000 from the practice, all the while sitting with the three other women in the family-like office, working day in and day out as if all was well. ▪

The fraud examiner has to consider the emotions of the people who have worked side by side with the suspect, day in and day out, as well as the emotions of the suspect's employers. At the onset, they will likely be in denial, as the doctor and practice manager in the above case were. They called counsel hoping for some other explanation – *It couldn't be theft, not her, not our small office.* Then, as they looked back at events over time, they felt violated, played, lied to, and used. At some point, as more details became known, they became angry, especially as more and more facts surfaced about the woman's theft scheme. As the puzzle pieces came together, so did their memories of their interactions with the woman throughout the years. They remembered the stories the woman shared and realized that some of them may have been made up.

We had another case where the company thought their CFO was a great guy who frequently flew to Florida to care for his ailing elderly parents. They were stunned when they learned he was actually using company funds to fly to Thailand to meet women. Then they realized that the person they thought they knew was a completely different person altogether.

In another case, a small business office had supported their coworker when she told them she was diagnosed with cancer. She lost her hair during her treatments, and the office held a fundraiser to help her and her family with their finances. The woman wrote and posted thank-you notes to coworkers in other departments, thanking them for rides to her treatments.

Later, when this woman was out of the office, traveling with her family on a cruise, her coworkers discovered that she had been stealing dollars out of the copier machine in the lobby of the public building. This led to a larger discovery that she had been stealing from their office as well, to the tune of $70,000. Worse, during interviews with others in the building, we learned from each person thanked in her cards that they had never driven her to any treatments, and several did not even know she had cancer. One witness stated that the woman had shaved her head and claimed to have cancer so that she could take more paid time off from work. The coworkers realized that when they had held a fundraiser for this woman, she'd never needed the money – she'd made the whole illness up. ▪

The fraud examiner needs to contemplate the emotions they will encounter when dealing with coworkers and supervisors, not just due to thefts, but also to lies. Violated, played, angry, resentful . . . all these words come to mind. Expect crying in all of the cases – plan for tears, and bring tissues to your meetings. Crying is discussed in detail later in the book.

OTHER OUTSIDE INFLUENCES – ALSO KNOWN AS "FRIENDS"

Another factor that can impact client emotions relates to outside influences that affect the client's decision-making process. An outside influence will most often be one of the client's closest friends, someone the client knows, likes, trusts, and confides in. These "friends" will be the ones the client turns to for what they believe is objectivity and honest advice. However, a problem frequently arises when the advice the "friend" provides is neither objective nor helpful, and in fact interferes with the client's ability to make independent decisions. We've worked hard on many, many client cases with a client's attorney, where collectively we were able to get the other side of the case to come to terms with what they did or at least understand that their actions have consequences. When that has happened, in nearly every case I remember, the opposing side made an offer to our client to resolve the matter. Many of those offers were good offers and included recovery amounts greater than the client would likely ever receive in other circumstances.

In these cases, we shared the offers with our clients, and it appeared the clients were going to accept and settle their cases. If only things could be signed and finalized right on the spot! When the client leaves the meeting or ends the call, you might think the case is over. However, an experienced fraud examiner knows that it's not over until the settlement is signed and accepted.

In many of these situations, the client calls the next day, all worked up, anxious, and apprehensive about accepting the offer. When I ask the client what happened since we last spoke, in many cases they state that they spoke with a friend and the friend told them they could do better. Of course, the friend provided that sage advice without any direct knowledge of the matter, without any experience in how these matters are resolved, and without any understanding of case's strengths and weaknesses. Yet somehow the friend has convinced the client they should not accept the offer and should continue to spend hundreds if not thousands of dollars on professional fees trying to get . . . well, in their friend's opinion, *more*. The friend seldom can articulate what they mean by this; they simply believe the client should be getting more.

In these situations, you will often have to be the voice of reason for the client, identifying the pros and cons of accepting the offer versus continuing to pursue *more*. I start with a strategy of educating my client about some hard facts. For example, only 5 percent of matters make it all the way through to a trial, and 95 percent of matters settle through various means or are dropped altogether. I then tell my client about the uncertainty of taking their chances at a trial, relying on a judge or jury to decide in the client's favor. In a court case, the verdict is out of the client's control. However, in a settlement, the client has full control over what happens. I tell the client that no one leaves a litigation or a settlement happy. However, the goal is to bring closure to the client's matter in a way the client can live with. Happiness is not the expected outcome; closure is the goal. Ideally, that goal will have been addressed at the initial meeting when I originally set the client's expectations. I remind the client that seldom is there justice, just a resolution to the matter. I try to be objective yet truthful. The decision to accept an offer or continue pursuing a case is solely the client's decision, and they will have to live with it.

By the end of our discussion, after the client has finished venting, I am usually able to bring their anxiety and apprehension back to a manageable level. However, now they are likely undecided as to what they should do, and in many cases, they express how tired they are of their case dragging on and on, as well as the toll it has taken on them. Many clients say they want to simply give up. Such a range of emotions is not uncommon from the start of these conversations to the end.

Here, the fraud examiner has an opportunity to really help the client so they don't leave the call or meeting in despair. Remind them that they have an offer they can accept, that they *can* get closure, and they *can* stop investing any further time, money, and energy into their matter. They can choose to move on with their lives, close the book on their case, and put it up on a shelf where they never have to revisit it again. As a result of these discussions, many of my cases ended with the client accepting the offer and achieving closure. The client wasn't happy – but they weren't going to be happy with the outcome, regardless of the path they chose to follow. No client ever is.

 DRAWING A LINE IN THE SAND

In some cases, the client chooses to use their matter as the event to address previous wrongs against them, and decides to take a stand on how their matter is resolved, even if it is contrary to what they logically should do. If a client feels they have received the short end of the stick all of their life, they may choose to use their actual or perceived leverage in their matter to obtain restitution for all the past deeds against them. This can especially be the case if the client feels they have been taken advantage of in the past, as was the case in the following matter.

W e received a call from an attorney representing a married couple involved in an estate settlement. The attorney and the estate were in another state, and the couple lived in the same town that my office was located in. The attorney provided us with a brief overview of the matter and said he needed to retain our services to help his client resolve the estate. A gentleman who was not related to the attorney's client had passed away and left his entire estate to be shared equally between his client and his client's brother, who lived near the gentleman. The estate was worth more than a million dollars. The client's brother had been named executor over the estate and had handled the deceased's funeral as well as his finances since his death. The client's brother had prepared the required estate inventory, listing the man's assets at the time of his death, and had also prepared an accounting, detailing income and expenses that occurred since the gentleman's death.

The attorney said his client and his wife were very angry with the brother and that they wanted to take him to trial, alleging that he had diverted some of the funds for his own personal benefit prior to splitting the remaining estate. The attorney said his client wanted to meet with me directly once we were retained for the engagement.

When the attorney finished giving us the background, he told us that the estate was being settled in a small town in his area and that the probate judge had little patience when dealing with disputed estates and distributions. He said the town was small enough that everyone knew each other and that he saw no value in some out-of-state beneficiary retaining a forensic accountant to investigate an estate, since the judge was not likely going to listen to the findings anyway. The attorney said he thought his clients were simply being difficult and that in the end they were likely to receive the amount identified in the brother's accounting. He ended by saying that it was their money and they could spend it any way they wanted.

We invited the couple to come to our office to meet and explain to us the issues that had prevented them from settling the estate and receiving their funds. The husband and wife were both in their sixties, and he was a long-time blue-collar worker who worked the second shift. The wife was a homemaker, and we quickly recognized that she was the speaker for this couple. She told us that her husband was slow at times and did not completely understand things, especially if they were explained too quickly. She told us she understood things and that they were tired of being screwed over their entire life. She said that when they bought their house, someone took advantage of them and that when they bought their cars, some folks took advantage of them. She said that all their lives, people had taken advantage of them, and that with this estate, they had decided to draw a line in the sand. Angrily, she said that they were not going to get screwed one more time, especially by her husband's brother.

I let her vent and gave her time to breathe and calm down. Then I calmly told her that I understood. I explained to her that this was the first I was learning of this case and that I wanted her to start at the beginning of this particular estate matter. I asked her to slowly walk me through what had happened and, more importantly, why she believed they were getting less than what they expected.

She explained that the gentleman who had died was someone who had no known family members and that, growing up, her husband and her brother-in-law had come the closest to being his family.

I wondered why she was providing this story when she hadn't even been there at the time and while her husband was sitting right across from me. Why wasn't he telling me the story? I sensed who was in control, and it wasn't him.

The wife said that her husband moved away to the town where he'd lived for the past 40 or so years, and that his brother had remained where they'd grown up. When the gentleman passed away, she believed that neither her husband nor his brother knew that he had named them as sole heirs of his estate (although she wondered whether her husband's brother had known about the inheritance all along). She described her brother-in-law as a wheeler-dealer who bought and sold properties, moving from one house to another, and she said that he had done very well for himself. She wondered if he simply ripped people off to build his estate, and she said he wasn't someone to be trusted. She described how she and her husband lived very modestly, leading a minimal lifestyle with little means to do more, and that it wasn't fair that the brother-in-law had done so much better than they had. She said they'd grown suspicious when they learned the brother had been named executor of the estate and felt he would use the opportunity to take advantage of them.

I asked them if they had ever been involved in settling an estate. They said that this was their first time and it had come as a surprise to them they were named as beneficiaries because they were not related to the man. I slowly explained to them how the probate process works and the court's expectations of the executor of an estate. I asked them why they thought they had been cheated by the brother.

The wife opened her copy of the accounting that had been prepared by the brother and pointed to the highlighted items. She pointed out expenses the brother had paid and explained how the items benefited him personally. She said he was not entitled to reimbursement for his personal expenses and that the items did not belong on his accounting. She said he shouldn't have included the items as reimbursements and that the expenses reimbursed to him made his share larger, reducing the remaining amount to be split equally between her brother-in-law and her husband.

While I agreed, based on the limited information I had seen, I told them I would need to review the financial activity in more detail before weighing in on their position. The couple agreed to continue my involvement in the case.

Through my procedures, I determined that certain parcels of land were designated to be distributed to the brother, and the brother had used his funds to make improvements to the land he was inheriting. Thus, he was making his parcels of land more marketable by using the estate's funds to reimburse his costs. I agreed with my clients' position that the brother was using his fiduciary position as executor to enhance the worth of his inherited assets. I also identified instances where the brother had requested reimbursement for personal expenses. The credibility of my clients' position was becoming clearer to me.

Through my analysis, I was able to identify over a hundred thousand dollars' worth of items for which the brother had requested to be reimbursed by the estate, prior to making the equal distributions. I shared my findings with my clients' attorney, and per his request, I once again met with the husband and wife to explain my procedures and findings. They seemed very pleased that my work supported their suspicions.

Several months later, I received a call from their very frustrated attorney. He said the brother had offered his clients a fair amount to reduce the brother's inheritance and increase his clients' share, but that his clients were being unreasonable and wanted to take the matter to trial. The attorney said that a trial in that little town was unheard of and that it would involve thousands of dollars in legal costs, including bringing me to the town to testify, and that his clients were crazy not to accept the offer. I calmly asked him if he wanted me to meet with his clients to help them reach a resolution, especially since they lived in my town. He said he would like my help. (I then recalled what he'd said in his first call, that retaining a forensic accountant was a waste of time and money.)

When I met with the clients, they were very angry. While the brother-in-law had brought the distributions close to equal, he was still getting a larger portion of the funds. This made the couple mad and reluctant to settle. They said they wanted to go to trial to show the judge and jury how the brother had ripped them off. I explained to them that I understood and that much of their life they likely had been taken advantage of (although I know some people go through life thinking everyone is ripping them off, even when that isn't reality).

I explained to them the likely costs involved in going to trial and showed them how the amount they were seeking was far less than the projected costs. I explained to them that, in most litigation matters, a settlement is reached between the parties and that a very small percentage (5 percent) of cases actually go to trial. I walked them through the calculations, both before the brother made adjustments to his accounting and afterward. I showed them that the amount they had been offered was within a few thousand dollars of what they sought. Their proposed distribution had increased by nearly $75,000, every penny of which the brother had not been initially prepared to give them. They had actually done very well in seeking their fair share. I then reminded them that being named as a beneficiary by the gentleman, someone who wasn't even related to them, was a major windfall, and that with each day's passing, improvements to their life were being held up as the funds remained in the estate pending resolution and distribution.

I asked them what it would take for them to feel they had won, for them to feel vindicated. I asked them what they needed so they could sleep at night, knowing they did everything possible to get what they were entitled. The couple talked between themselves for a moment and said they wanted another $1,000. I told them I would see what the attorney could do for them, and then they left.

I called the attorney, updated him on our meeting, and shared that the couple would settle if the brother would allocate $1,000 more to their distribution. He thanked me and told me that the couple had been driving him crazy with calls, lengthy emails, and continued resistance to settling. He said he thought he could make the deal happen, and within a day he called to tell me the brother had agreed to allocate the additional $1,000 to settle the matter. I used the opportunity to remind the attorney that spending money on folks like myself often pays dividends in resolving matters. He said he agreed and thanked me for my help in resolving the estate.

The couple's efforts paid off, and they received over $76,000 more than the brother had intended to pay them. That was a big win for them.

The attorney allowed me to call his clients and share the news. In that call, I reminded them that they had won, that they hadn't let someone take advantage of them in this transaction. I told them this was a sign, a turning point in their lives. Then I told them to sign the paperwork when it arrived, deposit the check when it was received, and do things that would make them happy with their unexpected windfall. They thanked me for my work.

A few months later, I saw that they had sold their small house and purchased a much larger historic house on Main Street. I truly hope they used the funds to make themselves happier people.

A fraud examiner, if doing his or her job properly, will find themselves in a position of trust with their client. Through listening, acting nonjudgmentally, providing objective feedback and advice, drawing on past experiences, and keeping the client informed, the fraud examiner can establish a strong rapport.

Because of this rapport, the client will often seek the fraud examiner's feedback and opinions when making decisions.

My goal in how I treat my clients is not to become their friend or get emotionally involved in their drama, but to be an objective, competent, and sage addition to the team they chose to help resolve their matter. I want to establish a rapport with them and have them trust me because of my experience in these areas, where I have focused so much time and energy.

In some instances, the relationship I created went so well that the client continued to call me long after their matter was resolved just to discuss some unrelated issue they were having and to obtain input and advice from someone they trusted. I have been fortunate to have a few former clients continue to call me to this day, just to say hello and provide me with an update on their lives, especially if they are in a better spot than when I last interacted with them.

In the next section of the book, I identify specific emotions the fraud examiner can expect to encounter during an engagement, from crying and anger to depression and despair, up through the worst possible outcome in any matter – suicide.

PART TWO

What Emotions Will Be Encountered?

CHAPTER FOUR

Identifying Client Emotions: Emotions You Will Encounter

 EMOTIONS YOU WILL ENCOUNTER

As I was thinking about all of the different emotions I've encountered on various engagements, in both victims and suspects, I started writing them down to see how many I could remember. Working from my notes, here is the list, in no particular order:

Powerless	Afraid	Upset	Excited	Sad
Apprehensive	Irritated	Desperate	Hostile	Confused
Angry	Anxious	Fearful	Suicidal	Hurt
Lonely	Disgusted	Surprised	Mad	Frustrated
Annoyed	Disbelief	Disappointed	Ashamed	Embarrassed
Responsible	Drained	Discouraged	Stressed	Depressed
Resentful	Speechless	Scared	Betrayed	Terrified

In the following sections and chapters I discuss many of these emotions in detail, and how each relates to a fraud examination. I also detail how fraud examiners can address and react to each one.

NERVOUSNESS

Any individual involved in a fraud engagement will likely be nervous; based on my experience, nervousness in and of itself is not a sign of an individual's culpability. A fraud examiner should expect that everyone they encounter in an engagement will be nervous. Nervousness is natural; the mere fact that a client has to meet with attorneys and a fraud examiner makes them nervous. In response, the fraud examiner should try to accomplish two goals: (1) ease an individual's nervousness, and (2) determine whether the individual is nervous in a general sense or nervous because they've played some role in the fraud being investigated. My preferred approach is to talk with individuals about their nervousness at the inception of our interaction. I try to put them at ease, and then I watch as our interaction progresses to see if their anxiety increases or subsides.

Nervousness can be coupled with profuse sweating, excessive body movements like bouncing legs and wringing hands, rushed speech, and other bodily reactions. In the following case, I encountered one of the most extreme cases of nervousness I've witnessed in my career.

We were contacted to perform a review of the financial activity of a local church. An anonymous caller had reported that the church's spiritual leader may have been misusing the church's funds, and the church had retained counsel to have the claim quietly investigated without the spiritual leader's knowledge. Working with counsel, we created a cover story for our involvement, which was that the church needed to have its recent financial report independently reviewed by an outside accountant. Under this guise, we scheduled a time to visit the church's administrative offices and requested that the financial report and underlying financial records be made available to us then.

Upon our arrival, the church's secretary greeted us and brought us into a conference room where stacks of financial records were piled. Shortly thereafter, the secretary introduced us to the spiritual leader, and we discussed what we needed to do in order to complete our financial review. The spiritual leader was very pleasant and offered any assistance he could provide. He then told us that he needed to go deliver a service and then do some errands. He stated he would be back later in the day to answer any questions we might have. He instructed the secretary to provide us with whatever we needed, then left the building.

Once he was gone, the secretary came into the conference room and sat with us. She told us that she was the one who had made the anonymous call and that the bank and credit card accounts that showed the suspicious activity had not been provided for our review. Only the spiritual leader had access to those records. The secretary told us that the monthly statements for those two accounts went directly to the spiritual leader, and she had no idea what happened with them after that point. Those documents were not maintained with all the other account statements.

The secretary then provided us with two months' worth of statements for those accounts that she had intercepted, photocopied, and then resealed and left for the spiritual leader. Upon a quick review, it was clear that the activity detailed in the statements was not church-related.

We went through the records that had been left for us and awaited the spiritual leader's return. When he arrived, we asked him to join us in the conference room. Once he was settled, we provided him with an overview of the records we'd reviewed in his absence. Then we asked him if there were any other accounts for which he had not provided statements. He stated that there were none, but we noticed that his demeanor changed, his face loosened, and he turned white in response to our request. We then asked him a second time if he was aware of any other bank or credit-card accounts that he had not provided for our review. He once again stated that there were none.

Then we showed him a copy of the bank statement and credit card statement for the two accounts for which he'd failed to provide records. His posture changed. He began to melt down into his seat and beads of sweat stood out on his forehead. We asked him if he was aware that the two accounts existed, and he said he was. We asked him why he had just told us there were no other accounts, when there were at least two others. He said he'd forgotten about those two accounts. We then asked him if he knew where the rest of the monthly statements were for the two accounts. He replied that he had them in his office. We asked him to retrieve them, and we walked with him to his office to ensure he didn't do anything with the statements except provide them for our review. He pulled two folders from his desk, both full of monthly statements. We then asked him to return with us to the conference room so that we could continue our discussion.

He followed us back, sweating profusely, and slumped back into his chair. We showed him the first monthly statement and asked him to explain each transaction, starting with the first, which documented a transfer of funds to an organization located in South America. As we questioned him, we observed that not only did his sweating increase, but also his legs bounced around and he began fidgeting with his hands. He stated that part of his clerical duties was to help other spiritual organizations in need and that the transfer in question was to one such organization. We continued down the list of reported transactions, many of which were personal in nature, and he provided story after story rationalizing why each amount had been spent. We asked him if any of the activity in the accounts was personal in nature, and he stated that he had explanations for each and every transaction.

As we discussed each transaction, it became clear to us that not only were the transactions personal rather than church-related, but also that he was lying about each one. We asked him if he would be able to provide us with supporting documentation for each transaction, and he stated he would, but that he would need time to pull his records together.

I noted that the more nervous he became, the more he started to pass gas, to the point I believed he could no longer control when it occurred. He was by far one of the most nervous individuals I'd ever encountered, and the more we delved deeper into his activity, the more nervous he became and the more he lied.

We stopped short of his collapse at the conference room table and told him that he could use his time wisely to gather up supporting documentation for all of the bank account activity as well as the credit-card charges. We copied all of the statements he'd provided, left copies for his files, and secured the originals. Then we left him to find the records we both knew did not exist.

The next day, I received a call from the spiritual leader. I asked him if he had been successful in locating all of the supporting documents for our review. He stated he was still working on that, but he was calling to apologize for misstating certain information during yesterday's meeting. He said he realized that not everything he'd said to us was factual and that he was taking full responsibility for his actions. I asked him if he was telling me that the activity we'd identified was personal in nature, and he said he was still working on that aspect. He provided no further details, and despite our repeated calls requesting the additional supporting records, he never scheduled another meeting with us. We drafted our report and findings, and he was subsequently arrested and prosecuted for embezzling the church's funds. ▪

Nervousness is normal and a natural reaction to being involved in a fraud examination. However, excessive or continued nervousness is something a fraud examiner should be watching for during interactions. As the interaction continues and the nervousness does not subside, or worse, becomes even more noticeable, the fraud examiner should make it a point to discuss why the individual is acting so nervous.

CRYING

People are going to cry as part of fraud engagements, so it's best to anticipate it, prepare for it, and embrace it when it happens. The most important thing to do in response to crying is to offer the person tissues and allow them some time to regain their composure. The key to successfully deploying this response is to be prepared, which means you have to carry tissues with you all the time.

At the beginning of my career, nothing in my training or education had prepared me for dealing with people crying. There were no discussions about this in any classes I'd taken for my criminal justice degree, and certainly the topic of clients crying never made its way into any of my accounting and taxation classes. However, looking back, tears and other client emotions should have been part of the curriculum.

For example, consider how clients react when preparing their federal individual income taxes. Not every client will be happy with the results on their tax returns, especially if they owe money or receive a significantly smaller refund than they expected. When first learning the results of their tax returns, clients easily become agitated, angry, depressed, confused, or frustrated – and the tax preparer will bear the brunt of their initial reaction. Often, the only effective strategy is to let the client vent and allow them time to recover. During this time, the tax preparer must stay calm and listen, rather than trying to explain. Once the client regains composure, or at least takes a few deep breaths, the tax preparer can start a dialogue, explaining the reason for the results as well as the available options, such as installment payments.

This scenario is real. Clients get upset when they have to pay taxes. However, nothing in any tax course I have ever seen has ever discussed how to deliver this type of news and react to the subsequent emotions. Clients become depressed and desperate when large sums are due and they realize they have limited or no means of paying the amount owed. I have had more than one client break down and cry once they started to process how they would not be able to pay their taxes and all their other expenses.

I could describe many scenarios beyond taxes that evoke emotional client interactions in other accounting contexts. However, no training or discussion exists to prepare accountants.

My point is that nothing prepared me for what to do when someone I was interacting with on an engagement started to cry. However, after my first experience with tears, when a woman I was interviewing for embezzling funds from her employer began to cry, I learned to never be without tissues. To this day, I carry tissues in all of my bags.

Responding to an individual being upset by providing them with tissues allows me to build a rapport with them, even if they have been difficult up to that point. Once I realized this phenomenon worked, I added this strategy to my approach, considering in each case whether getting the person to cry and offering them tissues would help move the case forward toward a resolution – not in every interview, of course, but certainly in interviews with individuals who were steadfastly denying their involvement or with individuals who were less than cooperative. What I found was that, although it didn't work every time, once someone broke down, recovered, and told me their story, they would then tell me that the weight of the world had been lifted by finally sharing the details of a secret they had been harboring for a long time.

One may ask how a fraud examiner goes about getting someone to cry. Well, there is no one answer, as each interaction is unique. One strategy I have used was taking the activity and actions and bringing them to a much more personal level. I asked them how they would feel if something like this happened to them, and what impact they thought their actions had on the victim, their family, and their life. I tried to get the individual to think about the impact and consequences, not only on them, but on others involved in the case. I asked them about their relationships, the impacts the case had had on them, and what those relationships would look like once the details became known about what happened. Sadly, fraud and financial crimes have been coined victimless crimes, which anyone who works in this area will attest is definitely not the case, and I use my interactions to show individuals that fraud does have victims.

I have also witnessed many instances where the person I wanted to meet with was crying before we even met, and I've had to begin our meeting by getting them to calm down. One meeting I remember involved a woman who was crying as she walked down the hall and into the conference room. She cried throughout the meeting and continued crying as she left. Nothing I said or did could get her to stop crying – and she was only a witness and not even the suspect in the matter!

In some cases, people cry to make another person feel sympathy for them. Not all crying is genuine, and someone looking to manipulate or distract can turn on the waterworks simply as a ploy (the term "crocodile tears" comes to mind). Experience will help you distinguish genuine tears from false ones.

As a fraud examiner, you should expect that people will cry – not just women, but also men. In my personal experience, I've often seen women cry, and so seeing them cry during an engagement did not surprise me. What did surprise me was the first time I witnessed a man cry during a meeting. For whatever reason, I don't recall any experiences growing up where I saw a man cry. Perhaps this was a part of my upbringing, with the thinking at that time being that men don't cry. At any rate, the first time this occurred during a meeting, I felt very uncomfortable and uncertain of how to proceed. The man in the meeting didn't have just a single tear running down his face; he broke down completely, face in his hands, bawling his eyes out. Since that meeting, I have witnessed this phenomenon many times, which may be a sign of the changing times. Men may express more of their feelings today than perhaps they did in the past. In any case, I am now better prepared for this situation.

Before meeting with clients, I recommend that fraud examiners perform a self-evaluation to determine what experience they have in addressing and responding to client emotions. For example, you may have seen an individual's eyes turn red and water, and witnessed a single tear run down their face. But have you witnessed an individual breaking down and wailing continuously? What training do you have to console the person, to allow them to cry up to a point, and then to start bringing them around to be able to continue the meeting?

For me, the best teacher has been experience. I remember some instances where I was in a meeting and someone else did a really good job dealing with an individual who became upset. In those cases, I learned from how they handled the individual. In other cases, I learned by how I handled the individual, and I focused on doing a better job the next time. It also helped that I have worked on an ambulance for 25 years as a volunteer emergency medical technician. In that context, I have had to console hundreds of individuals in a wide variety of situations where much more was at stake than potential fraud issues. There, too, I learned from other providers much more experienced than myself, and in each interaction I learned how to better handle the next one. I learned the importance of remaining calm, speaking in soft tones, and empathizing with the individual. I learned to listen more than speak, and I continue to practice that every day.

In dealing with weeping individuals, my advice is simply this: Let them cry. However, in addition to giving them space to weep, you should also control the interaction, offer consolation to end the crying, and then steer the conversation back to why you are meeting with the individual. The following case illustrates the emotional impact fraud can have on individuals, especially when family members are involved and are responsible for the fraud.

We were engaged to conduct a fraud investigation involving a family business originally started by the father. Upon his passing, his three sons continued operating the business, while their sister was responsible for all of the financial aspects, including collecting the revenue and paying the bills. One of the brothers was in charge and made many of the operational decisions. The other two brothers, who were also owners, were much less involved in the day-to-day activity. The children's mother was not involved in the business but was very much involved in her children's lives, especially the lives of her daughter and her daughter's son, both of whom happened to live with the mother in her house. There was a fourth brother who was also part-owner of the business, but he ran his own independent business within the same industry. There was a high level of animosity and sibling rivalry in this family, especially between the brother running the family business and the one running his own independent business.

For years, the family business had done very well, and each family member made a decent living from what they earned. The sister handled the accounting functions and ensured that tax returns were filed, and her brothers ensured that the business remained viable and profitable.

If that had been the end of the story, everyone could have lived happily ever after. However, that did not remain the case for this family. After a while, the brother who primarily ran the business put more and more time and effort into his responsibilities and requested that his compensation be adjusted accordingly. His request created quite a stir within the family, especially with the brother who had his own business and with the sister who handled the accounting. When they refused to provide him with an increased salary, he asked to inspect the business's books and records to see why an increase could not be made.

His request to review the bookkeeping and accounting records was met with a firestorm of delays and denials by his brother and his sister, creating more and more anxiety and resentment. Predictably, the brother and sister who were in conflict involved their mother in the situation, which complicated matters further and did not provide the brother with access to his requested information. The brother, along with the two brothers who also worked in the family business, retained an attorney and initiated a claim against his brother and sister in order to get court-ordered access to the books and records. The situation had now escalated to where the three brothers had to file suit against their other siblings. The family was now divided, with the mother supporting her daughter and the son who ran his own business.

Through much legal effort, the three brothers gained access to the business's bookkeeping records and bank statements. We were retained to review those records and determine why there had been so much resistance to providing them.

As you can imagine, it did not take long to discover that the sister had been using the business's funds for her own personal gain. She had paid herself bonuses, paid for personal expenses through the business accounts, and used the business credit card for personal purchases. Furthermore, she had used the family business to process and pay some of her brother's unrelated business expenses – which explained why that particular brother had aligned with his sister.

The schemes were simple, and the evidence was obvious. We identified and quantified the personal and unrelated business expenses and scheduled a meeting with the sister to obtain her explanation.

When she arrived, she was very matter-of-fact. While she wasn't outright angry, she had an edge to her. I started the conversation by explaining my background and what I had done with the records to date and identifying those things for which I needed her help to clarify and understand. As I was working toward establishing a rapport, she abruptly stopped me and told me she knew what this was about. She said she knew who I was and that I was very good at what I did. She said she knew that I would want to talk to her about the bonuses and personal changes. Then she asked me if I wanted to know what it had been like for her, working all those years for the family business and what she had to do to make it all work. I recognized a golden opportunity for her to provide me with much information, so I asked her to tell me her story. And she did.

As she told her story, she reached parts where she got so mad that she turned bright red and looked as if she wanted to punch the wall. At other times, she simply started to cry. I felt like I was watching her ride an emotional rollercoaster. She was happy when she spoke about the good times she'd shared with her now-deceased father and her brothers, then she turned resentful when relating how her brothers were doing better than she was while she worked harder than any of them. One moment, she would be about to pound her fists on the conference room table and the next she would be crying into her tissues.

By the end of the meeting, we had accomplished our goal. The sister had acknowledged the bonuses and other transactions that we identified. She thanked us for the meeting and to listening to her side of things. Then she left.

Allowing her to express her emotions and tell her story on her terms allowed us to more easily access her story and to get her to acknowledge her wrongdoing. Creating an opportunity for individuals to share their story based on the uniqueness of each case can often lead to building a rapport with them, and then to them sharing the details of their actions they may not have otherwise provided.

The case dragged on for quite a while, but in the end the siblings ended up settling the case without having to go through a trial. The ironic part of this case was that we saw the woman in our parking lot and on the floor of our building visiting another business on several instances after our meeting, even after the case settled. In every instance we crossed paths, she never acknowledged us or made eye contact.

It is not uncommon that someone is embarrassed about their actions or that they broke down during a meeting, and it is also not uncommon that someone seeks avoidance versus interaction the next time our paths cross. We try not to take it personally, and remind ourselves that we were just doing a job to resolve a matter.

ANGER AND HOSTILITY

When looking at all the different emotions a fraud examiner witnesses on a case, crying seems much more controllable than anger and hostility. Individuals involved in fraud engagements and other forensic accounting matters, such as divorces, bankruptcies, and family and business disputes, are typically under a lot of stress. The mere fact that they will be interacting with a fraud examiner causes them stress. Emotions often run high in these engagements, and both anger and hostility are common. An individual's anger may be consciously directed at the fraud examiner, or the fraud examiner may simply be in the wrong place at the right time. When meeting with someone who is likely involved in fraudulent activity, the fraud examiner should expect that the person may use anger to distract or deter the fraud examiner from focusing on them. The person may also use their physical presence to intimidate.

When individuals are under stress and become angry, they can become loud and even shout at times. The fraud examiner should be prepared for the individual to swear, lash out, and even throw objects. I have seen pens, pads, files, and even a telephone thrown across the room – fortunately, never in my direction. But I also know where to sit during a meeting to maximize my safety and minimize personal risk. I assess every room and identify the paths available to leave the room if needed. I sit near the exits, and never in a seat that is boxed in based on the room's configuration. I also never sit with my back toward a door. A whole book could be written on the subject of how a fraud examiner can best ensure their personal safety while conducting fraud examinations.

The main strategy a fraud examiner should utilize is keeping the individual's anger at a level that is manageable. In other words, the fraud examiner should not allow emotions to escalate to the point where violent outbursts happen. Just like a law enforcement officer who is trained on how to de-escalate a situation, the fraud examiner needs to recognize when someone is getting angry and then prevent that person from getting even angrier. Taking a break from the meeting to allow things to cool off or ending the meeting completely may be the best option. Meetings can always be continued at a later time, but if things get out of control and, heaven forbid, someone is injured as a result of the meeting's continuation, the consequences may not be easily reversed.

The fraud examiner should expect that individuals will become angry. Individuals may be angry for putting themselves into a certain situation, or they may be angry with others they feel are responsible for their situation. In a few instances, I have experienced an individual being angry with me personally, but in most cases, they were angry with me as the person tasked with holding them accountable. (The adage "Don't shoot the messenger" comes to mind.)

When I encounter angry people, I often resort to measures to de-escalate their anger, downplaying the severity of their situation and taking the time to explain to them who I am, what I'm working on, and what I'm seeking from them. I then open up the dialogue with big, open-ended questions like "What questions do you have for me before we start talking about things?" or "I want to be transparent and honest with you during our meeting, so feel free to ask me questions as we go through things." I want them to feel empowered and to redirect some of their anger into their own agenda for the meeting. I have my agenda, and I know I will cover everything I need to in our meeting, but often by giving them an opportunity to make this their meeting as well, I obtain a much better rapport and experience a vastly better exchange than if I had simply questioned the person.

However, in some cases, it is not to the fraud examiner's benefit to allow an individual to speak. In some cases, it's important to take control of the situation and let the individual in question know who's in charge. A recent case exemplifies how to take control of someone who has previously demonstrated anger and hostility.

We were engaged to meet the business manager of a school to determine how she accessed various systems, where she maintained financial records, and other aspects of her job responsibilities. Prior to the meeting, we had been told she was an angry person, and that members of management had requested this information from her in the past but she'd refused to provide it. Over time, by design, she had transformed her position into one where she had sole control of the accounting systems as well as all the financial and payroll-related information, and she was determined not to share that information with anyone.

We planned for an unannounced visit to the school, on a morning we knew the business manager would be at work. We waited until she arrived and got settled, and then we entered the school. Unbeknownst to her, we waited in a conference room while another employee went to bring her down for what she thought was a budget meeting. As she entered the door and saw us, her face dropped. She turned to walk out, but I called out to her, asking her to sit down. I told her that the school's president had directed her to meet with us.

I then introduced myself and my colleague and told her we had been engaged to help resolve some accounting issues. She laughed when she learned we were forensic accountants, and she was surprised when I shot right back at her, asking her why she'd laughed. She paused and had no response. It was clear to us she was not happy to be surprised by the meeting, which was an ambush by design.

Rather than immediately beginning my questioning, I asked her if she thought she had been ambushed this morning. She said that she did. I told her that that had been by design – specifically, my design – because we wanted the meeting to be a surprise. I don't think she was expecting me to be as direct with her as I was. I then told her that we were aware of her recent resistance to providing information and that the purpose of this meeting was to get those issues resolved. She stared right through me as I talked, and I could tell she was boiling with anger. I made a decision not to let her vent or address her growing anger, but to proceed, staying in control of the meeting and asking her questions that needed to be answered. When she provided vague responses, I pressed her for specificity. When she would say something like, "There are passwords to access the systems," I would ask her for the specific passwords, writing them down as she spelled them out. The tone I was working hard to maintain was that she was not in control; I was. She was an "at-will" employee, and her defiance and insubordination were not going to be tolerated.

We continued asking her questions and soliciting information for an hour or two. At some point, I asked her if she had any questions or wanted to say anything about the meeting or anything we had talked about so far. As she narrowed her eyes and focused, I told her she would have the chance to express herself, but for now we were going to continue with my questions. I knew this would not sit well with her, but I continued asking questions and getting the information I needed. I knew from what we had been told that she liked being in control and creating barriers for anyone who approached her. I wanted her to know that she was not in control here and likely would not be in control after the meeting. At times during the meeting, her face turned red and her brow furrowed, and she stared me down pretty much the entire time, but she continued to answer questions and we obtained all of the information we needed from her.

Once I knew my agenda was complete, I asked that we take a few moments and sit in silence as I reviewed my notes to ensure that we had covered everything. That was a ploy. I just wanted her to sit there as I flipped through my notebook, while she watched and wondered what I was doing. When I finished, I once again asked her if she wanted to discuss anything. Once again, before she could start talking, I told her I had two final questions. I asked her why she had acted the way she had prior to our involvement and also how she thought things could move forward with her and the school now that we'd had this meeting. She said nothing. I followed up by telling her it was sad that we were needed, and I thanked her for answering my questions. I told her we appreciated her spending time with us to educate us on how things worked with the school's finances. I then provided her with a business card and told her to contact me if she wanted to discuss anything further. I knew this would anger her, as she had been sitting for two hours, brewing with anger, answering questions, just waiting to tell us what she thought of the whole thing, and when it came time for her to tell us what was on her mind, I merely thanked her and ended the meeting.

Now, this strategy wasn't random, nor was it one I frequently use. It was calculated. I knew this woman was an angry person who wanted control and that everyone she worked with feared her. Unfortunately, that is not how things should work, and the school had already decided she needed to go, but not before all the information she was holding hostage could be obtained. We hadn't been engaged to listen to what she had to say. We had been engaged to solicit the information the school needed to move forward without her, and that is why I structured the interaction the way I did. That approach turned out to be successful.

It was clear to us she was very angry as she walked out of the conference room. I also knew that she was not expecting what happened next. She was placed on paid administrative leave, and she walked off the premises with only her pocketbook, car keys, and jacket. Everything else remained in her office with the promise that any personal items would be delivered to her house by an independent courier. We did not want to put anyone related to the school in potential jeopardy by having them interact with her during a delivery. The woman was subsequently terminated. ■

In this case what was important to the organization was for us to get the information from her that the organization needed in order to move forward without her, information that previously she would not provide to anyone, including her superiors. What wasn't important or a goal of our involvement was learning what she had to say about things, and so we chose a strategy that put us in control, extracted the information from her, and then ended our interaction.

In some of our cases, we knew in advance that the anger and hostility levels were so high that we would have to use additional measures to ensure our safety. In those cases, we worked with independent consultants (retired career law enforcement officers) who accompanied us on these matters. I credit their presence during those meetings for the lack of anger or hostility we faced during our involvement.

In cases that involve potential hostility, the fraud examiner once again needs to do an honest assessment of their personality, experience, training, and demeanor, and decide what they need for a particular matter. They should also seek out others who can work alongside them to complement their skill set. It is rare that one person has the sufficient training and experience to be able to handle all aspects of an engagement on their own.

 ## EXPECT SWEARING

A brief word about swearing: Depending on the fraud examiner's upbringing and beliefs, they may have varying levels of comfort with swearing. In my personal experience, I started working in a program alongside law enforcement when I was 14 years old. While I had not heard a lot of swearing in my house and was punished by my parents for using bad words, when it came to working with the police, I heard a lot of foul language. It became a second language to me, just part of the job. However, that experience was specific to law enforcement. I was raised in a religious household, where we attended church weekly. Swearing was not allowed in our house or anywhere else, certainly not at church or in Sunday school, which I attended for eight years.

My past experience with swearing came into play when I had my first case involving a member of the clergy. A clergyman had been accused of using the parish's funds to live a lavish lifestyle. I was forewarned that this individual, although he dressed in traditional clergy attire, had a terrible anger problem and swore a lot, using the worst words possible. I thought that information had prepared me for the meeting, but it hadn't.

At first everything was nice and chatty: "Yes, Father," and "How can I help you, my son?" But once we got into the substance of the meeting and his improper actions with the church's funds, everything changed. His anger came out, and he used the "f-bomb" over and over. Honestly, it blew my mind. I thought back to all the sermons and lessons I had been brought up with, and all the Saturday confessions I'd attended after using swear words, and now I was sitting across from a member of the clergy, hearing these words thrown about frequently.

SWEARING CAN LEAD TO HOSTILITY

During an engagement, people will swear – some constantly, and others less frequently. You should expect this, even from individuals you might not expect it from.

I want to end this discussion about anger with a story about an individual who was one of the angriest people I have interviewed to date. She was an embezzler who had been caught stealing from the company of which she was president, and she swore a lot.

An attorney representing the stockholders of a small business contacted me about the need for a fraud investigation. The attorney provided us with a brief explanation of the situation, and we set up a meeting at the company. The attorney stated he would be present, as would the business's existing management group members.

At the meeting, we learned that the company's president, together with her mother, was responsible for the accounting and finances of the business, with little to no oversight from or interaction with the other stockholders. The president, whom I will refer to as the daughter, came into the position when the last president had been removed from the company for embezzling. Now she was on the stockholders' radar, since they'd discovered evidence that she and her mother were using the company's funds for personal expenses. The stockholders had elected to place the mother and daughter on administrative leave pending an investigation into their financial activities.

The stockholders told us that, until recently, the mother and daughter had kept the financial records and details secret from others and had provided limited information on an as-needed basis. It wasn't until the stockholders independently obtained copies of the company's bank statements that they had the means to review the actual financial documents and activity.

Their goal was simple – identify all the transactions that constituted use of their company's funds for personal expenses. Counsel would use those findings to file a lawsuit against the mother and daughter for, among other things, theft and breach of fiduciary duty to the company and fellow stockholders. The stockholders were angry, since this was the second time in a few years that they had to address their president stealing from the company.

During the meeting, they described the mother and daughter to provide us insight into what it would be like when the time came to deal with them directly. They said the mother was older and not in good health. She collected Social Security while working part-time. They said she was the primary bookkeeper for the company and that she would do whatever her daughter told her to do. She would not likely meet with anyone unless her daughter was involved in the meeting.

The stockholders described the daughter as a bitter, angry woman who demanded to get her way and who treated people poorly. She was a miserable and vindictive person in the office and often screamed at her coworkers and fellow stockholders. The stockholders referred to this woman as toxic. They said that since she has been placed on leave along with her mother, it was like a heavy weight had been lifted from the company. The office environment was calmer, friendlier, and less stressed.

After accepting the engagement, we obtained business records for several years, including bank statements, credit-card statements, and paid invoices. As we reviewed the documentation, we highlighted the activity and transactions that did not appear to be business-related, such as cell phones for the daughter's family members (who did not work at the business), restaurant charges (on days that aligned with personal events in the daughter's family), and store purchases on the company's credit cards. Once identified and highlighted, we accumulated the identified activity onto spreadsheets and totaled the amounts. We maintained the highlighted documents to support our spreadsheet and provided counsel with drafts of our analyses. The attorney and the stockholders now had a basis to file suit against the mother and daughter.

Month after month, we received calls from stockholders, asking for an update. We directed them to their attorney, as our work was completed pending additional records to be provided to us for our review. As time went on, the stockholders grew more and more anxious and frustrated. The mother and daughter had been rallying support from some stockholders and were preparing to maneuver into a position where they could control a majority and then put themselves back into their positions. Frustration grew into franticness, and we received regular calls and emails from stockholders, asking us why things were taking so long. With each contact, I had to explain to them how the process worked and to ask for them to be patient, which was not an easy ask when they were faced with the possibility of having a toxic boss return to the company in a position to wreak havoc on everyone's lives.

Eventually, court dates and hearings became more meaningful, to the point where a judge attempted to mediate a solution to the matter, permanently separating the mother and daughter from the business but having the company compensate them for their stock. We were never part of any of the court hearings or the mediation.

The daughter's attorney came to our office to review our analyses. He was someone we knew from previous cases, and we had a good relationship with his firm. His review was very straightforward, and later in the case we learned he'd told his clients to settle the matter. I trust he knew that the activity we identified was sound and supported, which gave him pause in defending his clients.

It was not until the daughter retained her third different attorney that matters progressed toward a mediation. We learned that during a court session the daughter had asked the judge if she could meet with us and review our work, with the goal of reaching a mutually agreeable position regarding the transactions and activity we'd identified. The judge granted her request, and the attorney coordinated a time for the daughter to meet with us. The stockholders also contacted us and reminded (e.g., warned) us about the type of person we were about to meet.

She arrived at our office alone to meet with me and one of my staff. She sat immediately to my left, leaving little space between us. Then she took out her phone and told us she was going to record the meeting for her attorney. I told her we were recording the meeting as well, which we did, using an iPad. We had been planning on recording the meeting whether she said something about it or not, and the recording had already been started when we saw her walking up the sidewalk to our office.

She then asked us if we'd brought all the supporting records, bank statements, payroll journals, and other documents to the meeting. I responded that I had not, as those records would have been too voluminous and also because no one had told us we needed to have those records at the meeting. That made her angry. She started yelling that we were lying and that we knew the records were supposed to be at the meeting. She became extremely unpleasant, and I could see the anger and tension building in her face, neck, and hands. She told us we were in violation of the judge's orders. I tried to explain to her that there were no judge's orders. The judge had granted a meeting, and we were there to meet. However, she didn't accept my explanation, nor was she willing to listen to reason.

I convinced her to stop packing up her things and to sit back down, because we could still make the meeting productive even if the underlying records weren't present. She disagreed but reluctantly sat back down. Then, she asked me who had prepared the first payroll analysis. I told her I had. She started on the first line and asked me where I had obtained the amounts. I told her, "From the detailed payroll journals." She fired back, referencing the journals that I had not brought to the meeting, saying how convenient it was that the records were not available at this time. She then started yelling again, stating we should go meet with the judge, to which I calmly responded that we could do that if she wished, but we should finish going through my analyses before returning to court.

She wanted to know why her payroll items were on the analysis, when the other stockholders' activity was not included. I explained to her that we had looked at the others' activity but only saw the extra activity and pay-rate issues with her payroll. That started her off on a screaming rampage, as she described our biased approach that focused solely on her and no one else. Over and over, I tried to calm her down, but nothing seemed to work. Each time I brought her back to a specific transaction on one of my schedules, she would go off again, and this continued for three-quarters of an hour, her anger and rage escalating the whole time.

At about the 45-minute mark, she once again started packing up her things as if to go. She was standing over me, angrily pointing her finger at my face and yelling. I had a pretty good idea about the type of person she had been when she was running the company. I could only imagine what it must have been like working for the stockholders to work with her on a daily basis.

As I had done throughout the meeting, I tried to calm her down by asking her why she was so angry. She told me over and over that I already knew why she was angry. I told her we could go through the schedules calmly and in detail and provide her with the supporting documents after the meeting. She told us we would certainly be providing her with the documents and anything else she wanted, because she had a right to see everything. I agreed with her, but she kept yelling.

As she went to leave, I asked her why she had spent so much time focusing her attention on her payroll schedule, when we had other schedules that identified her personal use of the company's funds and credit cards. She shot back that she wasn't there to discuss those items. I told her I disagreed, that when the judge told her she could meet with us to review our schedules, that included all of our schedules. She snapped back that she wasn't at the meeting to discuss those items. I figured that since she was not going to behave reasonably, I would give her some insight into what was coming her way. It was a calculated risk, one that could have resulted in her leaving or punching me before walking out. However, I wanted her to know we had identified the personal activity that she wouldn't discuss and that it wasn't going to simply go away.

Remaining calm, I put the schedules on the table and asked her why her family all had cell phones paid through the business, month after month. She replied that I didn't know what I was talking about and that those family members worked in the business. I asked her why the large restaurant charges aligned with birthdays and holidays celebrated by her family. She had no answer. I asked her why there were store purchases on the business cards, and she said they were gifts. Then she said she wasn't going to talk about any of the activity, as that was beyond what the judge ordered. I reminded her that there was no court order, but that my questions were exactly what the judge wanted me to ask, to solicit her explanation of the identified activity. I told her that if she could clear up some of the items, we would remove them from our analysis. At that, she started to scream again. She told me she knew what I was doing and that she wasn't going to answer any more questions. Then she walked out of the conference room.

We watched her walk to her car, back out of her parking space, and speed away from our building. I thought about how dangerous it was to have someone so angry driving a car into traffic. I was truly glad she was gone and that the meeting was over, but I dreaded having to interact with her in the future. My staff member told me that during the meeting she'd thought several times that the woman was going to hit me, because she'd become so angry and hostile. I had never thought I was at risk of being assaulted, but after listening to the recording of our meeting, I realized how angry the woman had become. Even as I write this, I vividly remember the meeting, likely one of the most hostile of my career. ■

In the end, the case settled, I never interacted with the woman again, and the stockholders fared well in the settlement. Each time I checked in with the new president, I learned that the company was doing even better than the last time we spoke and had more cash flow than ever before in the company's history. I trust that these developments were no coincidence.

We have done things differently on subsequent matters to better prevent the level of hostility that we experienced, or at least be better prepared to react to it. There is a fine line between someone who gets as hostile as the woman did in this case and the individual turning violent. The woman in this case could have easily struck me or my staff member, or thrown things at us. The room was much too small, and there would have been limited means to react if she had turned violent. We learn from our experiences, and build considerations into future interactions to the extent that we can.

The next chapter discusses more anticipated client emotions, as well as one emotion that I did not anticipate and that created a unique set of issues on an engagement.

CHAPTER FIVE

Identifying Client Emotions: Disbelief, Betrayal, Resentment, and Excitement

DISBELIEF, BETRAYAL, RESENTMENT, AND EXCITEMENT

In my experience, there will be overlap in the many emotions a client feels during an engagement. All too often their matter involves family members, close friends, or longstanding employees. There is trust within these relationships, and when that trust is violated, it is often hard for the impacted individual to believe the violation actually took place. Denial is common, and you'll see it not only in victims but also in suspects. In many of my initial meetings where I shared my theories with a suspect, the suspect said things like "You're wrong" or "There's no way." Sadly, my theories almost always turned out to be accurate.

DISBELIEF AND BETRAYAL

Disbelief and betrayal are especially common when matters involve family members. I've witnessed this not just in divorces, but also within other types of family conflicts. It is often hard for the client to wrap their head around the fact that one of their family members did something to harm another family member.

Here's a brief example of a case that shows how betrayal can affect family members during an engagement.

A father had started a restaurant, and his three adult sons worked with him in the business. One son ran the kitchen, while another was the pastry chef. The third son ran the front of the house, meaning he was responsible for the customers, the dining experience, collecting and processing customer payments, managing the bar operations, and everything beyond food-related responsibilities. The third son also managed the business's financial records with his father. When the father passed away, this son continued doing these activities on his own.

Each brother drew a decent salary from the restaurant, and the brothers shared in the quarterly profits via a bonus check. As time went on, the restaurant did very well, and so did the brothers. However, the brother in charge of the finances appeared to be doing much better than his brothers. He'd moved into a large new house and purchased a new car, and his children had started attending college. The two other brothers were also doing well, but not on the same scale. They started asking their brother how he was making things work so well with his personal finances. The brother told them that his wife had been doing well in her job and her income made a big difference. However, both the brothers knew their sister-in-law well – they knew she'd never attended college, never held a full-time job, and only worked in hobby-type positions. When the two brothers asked their wives what they knew about their sister-in-law's employment, they learned that she had taken a part-time job at a daycare center.

Now suspicious, the two brothers met outside of the restaurant and discussed the situation. They decided to ask their brother for access to the restaurant's financial records. When the brother in charge of the finances refused them access, they began to get angry and resentful. They suspected that their brother had devised a way to get money out of the business without their knowledge. However, the more they requested information from their brother, the less forthcoming he became. Predictably, the sibling relationships deteriorated, making it more and more difficult for the brothers to work alongside each other at the family restaurant.

One day, the two brothers came to the restaurant as usual, only to find that the locks on the doors had been changed. They called their brother, who informed them that they no longer worked at the restaurant. The two brothers then called an attorney, and thus the formal division between the siblings began. The brothers became even more resentful toward their brother, as they had been equal partners in the restaurant but were now temporarily locked out and receiving no income. (Sadly, I have seen many similar cases over the years.)

Stunned and angry, the two brothers met with their wives and talked about their conundrum. Eventually, they determined there was no good solution to the matter. The two brothers would never go back to work with their brother, and they lacked the experience to run the other aspects of the restaurant on their own. The two brothers decided their only option was to find jobs at other restaurants while the legal process played out and they sought to hold their brother accountable for his theft. ▨

The fraud examiner may be in the unique position of recognizing what likely happened in a particular scenario early in a case and helping the client recognize the significant of what happened. The fraud examiner may help the client come to terms with the reality of the situation and, together with counsel, offer practical advice and direction. In this case, spending weeks or months trying to get the brother to change his course of behavior and make amends with his brothers was not likely going to be productive. Therefore, a more realistic path toward a resolution was to initiate a case against the brother and use the strength of the courts to gain access to information and ultimately resolve the matter.

If you're wired anything like me, you're wondering how a family member could do something like this to his own relations, knowing the hardships and issues they'd face as a consequence. I have found it truly sad to witness these types of cases, and I attribute these individuals' actions to greed, selfishness, and, in some cases, arrogance. In many of the cases the fraud examiner will learn the hardship the fraud has created, and will witness the emotional impact the fraud will have on the individuals directly and indirectly related to the matter, as was the case with the following case.

A woman contacted us asking us how she could retain our services. We asked her to tell us why she felt she needed the help of a fraud examiner. We told her to only provide a broad description of the issues, because until we were retained directly by an attorney on her behalf, there was no privilege over our conversation. She said she understood, and then told us that she and her husband were co-fiduciaries, each having a power of attorney over the same woman, a friend of their family. She'd recently learned that her co-fiduciary, her husband, might have done something inappropriate with the woman's funds.

She had never had access to the friend's financial records. However, recently she'd helped the woman sell her house and had gone to the bank with the woman to deposit the proceeds check received at the closing. The check was for over $200,000, and after the deposit was made, the woman's bank account contained well over $300,000.

At the time of the closing, the co-fiduciary, her husband, had been traveling for business. While he was away, his wife opened a bank statement that had historically gone directly to her husband and noted that the woman's account had a very small balance remaining. The wife knew the account had a significant balance after the house sale, and she could not explain where the funds had gone.

Our potential client talked very quickly and anxiously. She was concerned because she was the woman's co-fiduciary. Although she hadn't been responsible for the reduction in the woman's funds, because she was a co-fiduciary she could be held responsible for the loss. We asked her if she had spoken to an attorney, and she said she hadn't. We asked her if she had access to the woman's financial records, and she told us that the woman's records were locked up in her husband's desk at their house. We asked her if she had confronted her husband about the bank account balance, and she said she hadn't. He was still away on his business trip.

We asked her what her husband did for business and where he was traveling. She said he often traveled for a month at a time and that she did not know exactly where he was. He provided sales training consulting, and it was common for him to travel and not tell her exactly where he was. He would provide her and their children with a cell phone number they could call to reach him. That was the only way they could connect with him while he was away.

When we told her that the vagueness of his business trips didn't make sense to us, she started to cry. She said that their marriage was in trouble, and she feared that he wasn't doing training on his trips, but rather was having an affair. She said that when he wasn't traveling, he worked out of their home, secluded in his office with his computer. She said he was doing day trading, but that she didn't really understand what he did since he kept all of their financial records locked in a file cabinet.

Her primary concern was for her and her children. If her husband had in fact taken the woman's money, she needed to protect herself and her children from the consequences of his actions. As she spoke, she continued to cry.

We told her that if her husband traveled to the same area for month-long blocks of time on a regular basis, he may have a second family at the alternate location. The "sales training consulting" was likely a ruse, an excuse to allow him to slip away. We told her it was suspicious that he could only be reached with the provided cell phone number and never provided the address of where he was staying.

We told her she needed to get an attorney involved. The matter needed to be brought to the probate court's attention, since that was the court with jurisdiction over the woman's affairs. Then, once the court was involved, financial records could be obtained to determine what had happened to the woman's funds and what funds remained for her use and care.

The wife retained an attorney and notified the probate court. The probate court then retained us to investigate the financial records of the conserved person. The probate court also suspended both conservators from performing any further duties until the matter was resolved. We requested court orders to obtain replacement bank statements and discuss the bank accounts directly with the banks. The probate court issued the orders, and after a brief period, we received what we needed.

We identified transfers out of the conserved woman's bank account into accounts that the husband used to trade investments. We noted that, once transferred, the conserved woman's funds were comingled with the husband's accounts. We identified monthly transfers totaling $660,000. We did not identify any transfers or deposits back into the conserved woman's bank accounts.

We provided an update to the probate court and, with their authorization, we referred the matter to the proper agency for investigation. We then held a meeting at the conserved woman's residence. In attendance was her attorney, the probate court judge, the agent, and myself. The judge asked the conserved woman about the transactions and her experience investing with her conservator. Sadly, the conserved woman had no information and likely didn't understand what we were discussing with her.

In working with the agent, we learned that the conserved woman was not the only person from whom the husband had transferred funds to "invest." There were several other victims in his scheme. The agency also confirmed that the husband had a second family in the country he frequented for training purposes.

When we shared that information with our client, she broke down crying. She said she had suspected he had been having some type of affair. That would explain his secrecy and the length of his trips. However, to hear it confirmed simply blew her mind.

The husband was arrested and charged with a number of crimes, including the theft of over $1 million from multiple victims. His attorney fought in court to prevent any discovery of his records, accounts, and assets, and rationalized that although his client may have been an unlicensed investment broker, he was not a thief. His attorney said that all the husband's investors knew he was trying to get them a better return on their money and that there was risk associated with his approach. As far as I know, the husband never apologized or took responsibility for his actions.

Eventually, the husband was convicted and sentenced to federal prison. However, his conviction did not end the matter for his wife, who had been the co-conservator. Not only had she lost her husband and the father of her children, but she could also be held responsible as co-fiduciary and have to repay the $660,000.

Suffice to say, when the woman learned she might be responsible for repaying the funds, she was disbelieving. Under fiduciary law, she was supposed to ensure that the funds were secured and only used for the conserved woman's benefit. Although she had not been directly involved in or aware of her husband's theft, she could still be held responsible for replacing the funds. (The woman was ultimately not held responsible for her husband's thefts.)

Over the course of an engagement, a fraud examiner should be prepared for the client's emotions to transition from disbelief and betrayal to resentment. This is especially common when the culprit in the matter will not take responsibility for their actions. Matters get even worse when a culprit starts to rationalize their actions or initiates meritless counterclaims.

RESENTMENT

Resentment is a powerful emotion, and some individuals remain resentful their entire life, never able to let go of how they were wronged. Unfortunately for the fraud examiner, the individual's resentment will likely become a significant factor in their case. It is important to recognize this fact so that when you talk with your client, you can remind them that resolving the issues at hand will not necessarily also resolve a lifelong resentment. The client needs to focus on the current matter and then seek professional counseling to help them work through the issues causing their resentment. In my experience, as long as the client continues to combine resentment with the current issue at hand, we can accomplish no resolution or closure.

Often, I draw a Venn diagram (overlapping circles) for individuals, with one circle representing their matter and the other circle representing their emotions surrounding the matter. I then show them how the circles have to be pulled apart in order to resolve their current issue. I find that doing this exercise helps the individual focus on the resolution that can be accomplished with the aid of the fraud examiner, versus the emotional resolution. I refer to this as separating the business issues from the emotional issues. We can help work with individuals to resolve the business decisions, but they will need to seek the help of other professionals to resolve their emotional issues.

In the cases I shared in previous chapters, I trust you recognized the instances where resentment set in. Resentment is especially common in the context of a divorce. In my experience, the parties involved in matrimonial dissolution cases are often loaded with anger and bitterness toward each other, which can make these matters very contentious and at times toxic to those who are working on the case. I remember one case in particular where resentment characterized many of the interactions.

We were engaged by counsel representing a women who had filed for a divorce. The attorney requested that we investigate the husband's businesses and tax returns to determine what the husband's true earnings were and whether he was hiding any undisclosed assets. We learned that the husband ran a family business that had been started by his father. After his father's death, his mother became the majority stockholder, although she had never worked at the business. The husband's brother also worked at this business and had gotten divorced a few years earlier. In his divorce, his spouse had used a forensic accountant to reveal all sorts of activities the brother and the family were involved in through the business and various entities. The brother's spouse received a decent judgment of income and assets as a result of the divorce. The family was very angry because of this turn of events and had vowed that something similar would not occur with the present pending divorce.

As we requested meetings and information from the husband, we encountered obstacle after obstacle. In some cases, he provided us with incomplete records, and in other cases, no records at all. Despite court orders to allow us access to the requested information, we continued to hit barriers. We met with the outside accountant for the business and he also provided no information, as he had been instructed not to answer any of our questions. It appeared the family had pulled out all the stops to prevent us from accessing any information of substance.

The mother and majority stockholder dodged her deposition by providing the court with a letter stating she was too fragile to appear. However, this letter was contradicted by the husband's testimony that his mother worked at the business every day. This obstructiveness continued right through our depositions and the trial. On several occasions, when things got heated or when we got close to identifying the business's true activities, bad things began to happen to our client. Her car was vandalized in her driveway. Her ex-husband showed up at her residence and threatened her. Incidents like this continued to occur, but the police took no action, claiming it was a civil matter.

The husband's attorney retained separate forensic accountants to provide the court with their version of the husband's financial picture, and then the forensic accountants testified against us that we did not have sufficient information to rebut their testimony and opinions. By design, the husband and their family perpetrated a fraud against the court, and they eventually succeeded.

Needless to say, our client's level of resentment toward her ex-husband and his family grew and grew, especially when she eventually received a much smaller award from the court as a result of all of their antics.

I am happy to say she went on to make a great life for herself, returning to school to earn her degree and starting a practice in the area that she loved. She is a true survivor, and I trust she is doing much better without her former spouse in her life. ▪

In this case the family's resentment towards both sons' wives who separately filed for divorce drove their actions. The family was determined not to let any of their wealth and fortune go to either woman, and relied upon lying, fraud, and deception to carry out their plan. All the fraud examiner can do is request any and all information that should be available given the situation, and review what is provided. Based on my experience, if a party chooses to hide, withhold, discard, or destroy information to prevent the fraud examiner from gaining access to it, there is little a fraud examiner can do about it, even with a court order directing the party from preventing it from happening.

Unfortunately, bad things happen to good people, and sometimes the person responsible is a family member or friend. This can lead to many difficult, negative emotions, such as resentment and bitterness. However, the next emotion I describe is a bit different, and one you may not expect to encounter on a case.

EXCITEMENT

I can honestly say I never expected to meet anyone on an engagement who was excited to meet me, an auditor and fraud examiner. Most people cringe when they hear the words *audit* or *auditor*. When people think of an auditor, they're most likely to conjure up an image of an IRS agent combing through receipts and looking at little details, trying to find additional taxes due, along with penalties and interest. In general, I believe people dislike auditors and resent having to undergo audits, regardless of the type or purpose. The audit process by its very nature is designed to review and challenge the facts and ensure compliance. I think a fair amount of animosity would be generated in anyone receiving a notice that they are about to be audited.

Therefore, when I first met with individuals who were excited about my profession, I found those circumstances to be very unusual. In the following case, a client became a little too excited by the activities fraud examiners undertake during an engagement.

> We had been retained by an attorney representing a dentist who suspected his employee had been stealing from his practice. When we first met with the dentist, he presented us with computer reports and spreadsheets that he'd created, showing transactions that he'd found. He was not angry, upset, depressed, or desperate. Instead, he was excited by

what he had found. He used the word *fascinating* several times during that initial meeting and subsequently throughout the investigation.

He'd identified one of his employees as the person he believed was responsible for the disappearance of the funds. He explained to us that he had hired this employee dentist a few years earlier, directly out of dental school. He explained that a new dentist getting hired into a practice right out of school was extremely rare. He said he had attended this employee's wedding and that her father had thanked him for providing his daughter with such a great opportunity right from school.

Our client said that he paid each of his employee dentists the same way. Each was paid one-third of the charges associated with the procedures they performed, on a biweekly schedule. He said he would generate reports from his medical billing system every other Saturday and use the total amount for each dentist to determine their compensation for that period. He simply used the total for each dentist and divided the amount by three – and that was the amount of each dentist's gross payroll. So far, everything he told us appeared very straightforward.

Then he told us that he had been working on a patient when he overheard the front desk take a call from another patient asking questions about their bill. When the dentist finished with his patient, he asked the front desk employee what the call had been about. His staff member told him that the patient had left at the end of last week with a printed statement reflecting a balance they owed. Then the patient had received another statement in the mail showing a different amount owed. The dentist asked his staff member to contact the patient and ask them to bring in both statements. The patient came to the practice as requested, and the staff member made copies of the statements.

The dentist compared the two statements and was puzzled. He went into his medical billing system and reviewed the transactions and history on the patient's account. When he saw the transactions, they made no sense to him. The patient had been seen, procedures had been performed, and the charges had been properly entered into the system on the day of the patient's visit. The dentist who had performed the procedures was identified on the transaction. However, subsequent transactions had been recorded for the same procedures, and on these transactions, the name of the dentist performing the procedures had been changed. There were further subsequent transactions posted where the dentist's name had been changed yet again, this time back to the original dentist who'd performed the procedures.

Our client started looking for other patients who'd had similar changes made to their accounts, and he found more. He couldn't yet explain the changes that he'd found, but he started to see a pattern in the transactions. The transactions that changed the dentist's name were typically entered late on a Friday, after the practice was closed. The subsequent transactions, changing the dentist's name back to the original dentist, were made early on Monday mornings before the practice opened. Once he noticed this, the dentist got really excited: He had a mystery to solve.

Our client found many more transactions in his other patient accounts. At one point, he started to figure out why someone would change the dentists' names back and forth. It dawned on him that the dentists' compensation resulted from a direct calculation based on the charges posted by individual dentists. He also found another pattern that made him even more excited, because he believed he was closing in on solving the mystery. When changes were made on late Friday afternoons, the changes replaced the original dentist's name with the name of the new dentist he'd hired right out of school. When the Monday changes were posted, the new dentist's name was changed back to the original dentist's name.

When the dentist matched up the dates of the changes, he recognized that the changed transactions coincided with payroll weeks, with the Friday transactions occurring before the Saturday reports were generated, and the Monday transactions occurring after the Saturday reports were completed.

When he figured out what was happening, he didn't do anything about it right away. Instead, he waited to see if he could catch his employee in the act. He watched her for two weeks and noticed that she was in the habit of wearing a white lab coat in the practice. She always had computer reports sticking out of her lab coat pockets. When she didn't have any patients, which was often because she was fairly new and was still building up her patient schedule, she sat in front of the computer in the central area of the practice.

At the end of the two-week period, after watching for the changed transactions to be posted in the system, he called the new dentist into his office and asked her about them. She said she had no idea what he was talking about and that she never used the computers since she was computer-illiterate. Our client was very excited to be conducting an interview of a fraud suspect and loved that she had lied to him – it just made the case that much more interesting. He told her what he had found and that he knew she was the only dentist who benefited from the changed transactions. She told him he was wrong, grabbed her coat, and left the building. She never came back, so he covered her scheduled patients for the rest of the day.

The next day when he came to work, he opened the top drawer of his desk to retrieve the keys that opened various locked cabinets. There, he found a handwritten note in the top drawer that had not been there when he'd left the previous night. The note was from the new dentist, saying that she was resigning from the practice. The note also accused him of harassment, sexual harassment, and creating a hostile workplace. He wasn't angered by these accusations; instead, he was excited. He called his labor attorney, who in turn retained my firm to help resolve the matter.

We worked with the dentist to review three years' worth of transactions and identified a way to export the transactions from his medical billing system into a spreadsheet. Once in the spreadsheet, we were able to isolate the transactions and quantify the amounts involved. We determined that the scheme involved the new dentist taking credit for work performed by the other two dentists.

During the investigation the owner, still excited to be part of a criminal investigation, performed more patient chart reviews and found three other areas where the new dentist had been paid for work never performed, as well as instances where the dentist did not charge for procedures she performed on her family and friends. The dentist also added procedures that she never performed and increased the amount of work she actually performed, both of which resulted in increasing the amount on the report generated for payroll purposes.

As we worked with the owner, a large part of our involvement consisted of containing his excitement. He wanted to call the media to tell his story and relate how he'd put all the clues together. We recommended that he not contact or speak with the media. He then wanted to speak at state and national dental conferences, to share his experience with his fellow dentists. We recommended that he not talk about the case while the investigation was pending. He then wanted to write a book detailing how the fraud had happened and how he'd discovered it. We recommended that he not write any books, as sharing too many details about his case could lead to creating potential unneeded liability or nuisances down the road.

The dentist was very excited for us to get the employee dentist's reaction to our involvement in this matter. We attempted to meet with the employee dentist on several occasions. As a last resort, we drove to her residence. She answered her door, but refused to speak with us. We asked her if she knew why we wanted to speak with her, and she said she had no idea. We offered to tell her, and she listened as we told her we worked on behalf of her former employer. She then handed us the name and phone number of her attorney and asked us to leave her property. We walked to the car and drove away. As we drove, we discussed how unusual it was that she had answered the door for strangers she'd never met, and yet she'd had the name and number of her attorney in her hand when she answered the door. We found that odd, unless she always answered her door with her attorney information in her hand.

In order to prove that the new dentist had changed the transactions, we used the date and time stamps on each transaction and looked for another source of information that could be used to show she had made the changes. We identified two sources: the alarm system in the practice office and the parking garage gate system. We asked the owner to request transaction-level reports for all activity for the past 12 months. The owner was so excited that his investigation was expanding into these new areas that he could easily be described as giddy. Surprisingly, he was not at all concerned about the money that had been stolen and how he was going to make up the difference to the other dentists.

We used the gate access card data and identified the dates and times on the report when transactions had been changed. We determined that the employee dentist was the only person who had been in the parking garage at the time the changes appeared late on Fridays. This was also true for the changes made on early Monday mornings. Only the new employee dentist's car had been in the parking garage when those changes were made.

We then used the alarm report to identify who had turned off the alarm on the days when changes were made. Once again, we identified the new employee dentist, since it was her alarm code used at these times. The owner was fascinated by the way we'd matched the transaction changes to the parking access and alarm reports.

To provide you the ending to this case, a criminal complaint was initiated against the new dentist, and the police knocked on her door. We asked them to go to her house to let her know that the matter wasn't simply going away and that she should have her attorney connect with the owner's attorney to start discussing how the case would be resolved. In the end, the new dentist obtained a mortgage and repaid the owner for all of the funds she'd diverted, which the owner used in large part to pay his other dentist employees. Although the owner reported the new dentist to state and national dental associations, to the best of our knowledge, nothing resulted from that. A short time after the case settled, we saw an advertisement in the newspaper for a new dental practice accepting new patients. It was the same dentist who had just repaid what she had stolen.

In most of my cases, the client encounters many experiences for the first time – for example, going to court, being involved in a legal proceeding, and needing to interact with the police. In the case of this client who was so excited to be involved in a criminal investigation, it was likely the only time he would depart from his daily routines and become part of an investigation. The novelty can prove exciting because of the "*CSI* effect," which I discussed in an earlier chapter. In cases like these, the fraud examiner should be prepared to guide the client through the investigative process and manage the client's excitement about their case. The fraud examiner needs to keep them from interfering with the investigation and also needs to minimize any additional risk they could create for themselves. In rare cases, your client will need daily reminders about the proper way to proceed.

Fraud examiners should be cautious about excited clients. Sometimes, you will not know just how excited someone is to be involved in an investigation, and their words or actions could really mess up their case. The following story illustrates how client excitement can become problematic. In this instance, we encountered an individual who self-deputized and injected themselves into one of our investigations, creating potentially serious issues.

An attorney representing a small manufacturing company called to seek our assistance with a new matter. Several years earlier, the company's sole owner had hired a controller. The owner now believed his controller had been stealing from his company. The controller rarely took time off, and if he did, he always locked up his desk and cabinets while he was away. The controller was now away on vacation, and a few of the individuals who worked with the controller had come into the owner's office to tell him they believed that the controller had been stealing. The employees all worked for the controller and had feared coming forward sooner because they were afraid of the controller's retribution. The employees used this opportunity to tell the owner what they believed the controller had been doing. Once his staff showed him the evidence, it was clear to the owner that his controller had been stealing from the company.

We had a conference call with the owner and his attorney, and we developed a plan to surprise the controller upon his return, confronting him with the transactions and activity. We planned to require him to turn over his keys, to place him on paid administrative leave, and to continue the investigation, searching for more evidence in his desk and cabinets. The attorney cleared this strategy, since no expectations of privacy were present at the office. The owner had keys to the controller's desk and cabinets and would use them if the controller did not relinquish his own. Either way, we would have access once we met with the controller.

The controller was due back in the office on Monday and was often one of the first people to arrive in the mornings. Another employee typically arrived earliest, when she unlocked the building and turned off the alarm. Since the business was over two hours away from our office, we agreed that we would wait until the controller had arrived at work. Once he was there, the owner would notify us and we would start driving to the business. The controller would start his day as usual, and when we arrived, we would call him into the conference room for a surprise meeting. We ended the call with the owner with this plan in place for Monday.

On Monday morning, just after I'd arrived at the office and before my staff had arrived, I received a call on my cell phone. The female caller was very excited and was saying, "I got him." I didn't understand who this person was or why she was calling, so I asked her what she was talking about. The woman said she worked at the business with the controller, and the owner had told her to call me on my cell phone when the controller showed up for work. I told her I understood, but I asked what she meant by "I got him."

The woman said she had been planning her actions all weekend. She said she arrived earlier than usual that morning and staked out the office's driveway and parking lot, waiting for the controller's arrival. Once the controller entered the building, she told him to follow her, directed him into the conference room where she told him he couldn't leave, and then locked him inside. She then called my cell phone to let me know the controller was there and wasn't going anywhere.

Suffice to say, I was floored. Who was this woman, and what was she doing? Our element of surprise was now gone, and she now had the controller locked in a room. I told her to do nothing further, to unlock the door, and to just wait for the owner's arrival. Since I'd never made it into my building that morning, I waited in our parking lot for my staff to arrive. Once they did, we headed out to the business. We had a two-hour drive ahead of us, which meant the controller would be at the company for two hours, hopefully with the owner and not locked in the conference room.

On our ride, we called the attorney, who was equally surprised by the turn of events. I was angry with the woman, who had messed up our plan for the investigation. She also created new potential issues for the owner in that she was holding someone in a locked room. The controller could bring criminal and civil actions against the woman and possibly the owner for wrongful imprisonment. The attorney called the owner and instructed him to unlock the conference room door if it was still locked, and to request that the controller remain there.

When we arrived, we found the controller sitting in the unlocked conference room, casually reading a book. He asked what this was all about, and we explained to him who we were and why we were there. Because we'd had no time to get set up for the meeting, we dove right into our questioning. After an hour or so, we took a break, and I left to speak with the owner while my staff member stayed with the controller in the conference room. A short time later, my staff member came to get me and told me that the controller was ready to take responsibility for all of the identified activity. We returned to the conference room, where he admitted he was responsible for the transactions. ▓

The woman's unpredictable actions based on her excitement not only jeopardized the element of surprise for us, they caused risks and exposure to herself, the owner, and the company. It is important that the fraud examiner share with the client the importance of staying with the plan and not straying to perform steps not contemplated. If things happened that were unplanned, the client would be wise to immediately contact their attorney and the fraud examiner to best identify how to react to whatever happened.

Although drifting a bit from client emotions for a brief moment, I figured you, like myself, would love to know what ultimately happened in this case, and therefore I share the following brief events leading toward a resolution in the matter.

After a few hours of meeting, the controller turned in his keys, his business credit card, and his company phone, and he left the building. We watched as he drove out of the parking lot and down the street. We then conducted a search of his desk and file cabinets, where we found blank prenumbered receipt pads and a large quantity of store gift cards. We matched up the receipts attached to the controller's expense reports to the numbering sequence of the pads in his desk.

The owner subsequently terminated the controller and accepted a complete repayment of the identified diverted funds as settlement of the matter. We learned that the controller had obtained the funds from his father-in-law to avoid being arrested and charged with theft.

The interesting thing about this case was how the controller was stealing the funds. He would purchase large sums of grocery store and gas gift cards and periodically award one to an employee for good work or reaching a work milestone. The staff estimated he gave out maybe 10 cards a year, yet his expense reports showed he'd purchased hundreds of the cards. We'd asked the controller about the cards during our meeting, and he had provided no explanation.

The most likely scenario we came up with is that the controller may have been having an affair and providing the grocery and gas cards to his lover in order to avoid leaving a financial trail, which could lead to someone discovering the relationship. He could also have been using the grocery and gas cards as currency for other illicit transactions, such as buying drugs. We never figured this out for sure.

A few months after the controller's termination, the owner sent me a link to a news release from a large manufacturing company. The press release expressed how excited the company and owners were to have hired a new chief financial officer. Their new CFO was the same person we had just investigated, except now instead of being the controller, he was the chief financial officer – a promotion.

The controller never brought any actions against the woman, the owner, or the company for being locked in a conference room. To this day all we know is that he sat down at the conference room table and read a book that he brought to the office with him. We are not aware if he ever even knew that he was locked in the room until the door was unlocked.

 ## EVERYONE HAS A STORY

If you have experience in the fraud field, then I trust you have similar stories to the one I just shared. When I worked on fraud engagements, I often met individuals with no relationship to the matters we were investigating who just happened to either work at the business or knew someone who was involved. Once word got out and people learned I was a fraud examiner, they all wanted to talk with me. They wanted to share their own stories, or talk about a relative who wanted to go into this field, or to get my business card. That's why I eventually stopped carrying business cards – I can't give out cards if I don't bring any with me. In the end, each individual just wanted to talk with me because of the excitement associated with the case. There is no hard-and-fast rule on who the fraud examiner should talk with, and who they can disregard. My experience has shown that although many of the folks who just wanted to talk and were unrelated to the matter had nothing to provide that was useful in resolving the matter, I have had experiences where someone told me of other things that were unrelated to the matter, which created new issues to be resolved. So like myself, the fraud examiner will just have to use his or her own discretion on deciding who to allocate time to meet.

In the next chapter, I discuss "the three D's" – desperation, despair, and depression.

CHAPTER SIX

Identifying Client Emotions: Indifference, Depression, and Despair

 ## INDIFFERENCE, DEPRESSION, AND DESPAIR

Another emotion a fraud examiner may encounter on fraud engagements is indifference. I have experienced indifference with victims as well as suspects, and each time it has surprised me. I was surprised when a victim wasn't angry that someone had stolen a large sum of money from them, and I was surprised when a suspect facing significant consequences seemed indifferent to being discovered. I can remember a matter or two where the suspect sat emotionless during our meeting, acknowledging their actions as I showed them transactions and activities I believed they were responsible for, and showed no anxiety or remorse about what they'd done. When I asked about their lack of reaction, they gave a response along the lines of "It is what it is," or "It's right there in black and white."

I've also witnessed indifference in attorneys who were representing suspects accused of committing fraud. Sadly, when these attorneys sat across the table from us and told us that they doubted someone would ever prosecute their client, I knew based on my past experiences that they were likely right. However, I also knew that what their client had done was wrong, and somehow their client needed to be held accountable.

The following case illustrates indifference on the part of the suspect's attorney, who recognized based on past dealings with clients involved with financial crimes that the facts are the facts, and the best course of action is to have his client cooperate with the investigation.

In one case, I interviewed a woman who had embezzled funds from her employer, a nonprofit agency. She acknowledged that the transactions and activity were her doing and that what she had done was wrong. When we finished our conversation, I recommended that she contact an attorney, since these cases are often best resolved with attorneys representing both sides of the matter. She asked me for a referral, and I provided her with the name of a criminal defense attorney I knew. A few weeks later, I received a call from the attorney, thanking me for the referral and asking if we could set up a meeting with him, his client, and the attorney who had engaged our services. I asked him if his client would be available to answer more questions, and he stated that she would cooperate fully with our investigation. He said that white-collar crimes were usually black-and-white situations: "It is what it is." He said that rather than make things more difficult and cause the victim to incur more costs through the investigation, he had advised his client to cooperate fully.

We met, and his client answered all of my questions. The attorney was indifferent to our findings and his client's acknowledgments as she took full responsibility for the identified activity. He later called and thanked me for treating his client respectfully, with an objective, nonjudgmental tone. His client was arrested and received accelerated rehabilitation, which is essentially a one-time pass as long as the individual stays out of trouble for two years.

Based on my experiences I recommend using indifference to your advantage when dealing with those you believe are responsible for the fraudulent activity. Have the individual share as much detail as possible about what happened, playing on their notion that it really doesn't matter. So what is the harm in providing all of the details if it doesn't really matter?

One case involving indifference, which I completed several years ago, still surprises me today. It involved a small professional firm that had fallen victim to a substantial employee embezzlement.

The firm's owners, who were husband and wife, first learned they might have an issue when their bank began to return their vendor checks for insufficient funds. The couple was surprised because they had always maintained a significant buffer balance in their accounts, so they started to look at their bank statements. Not having any accounting background, they called their attorney, who in turn recommended that they retain our services.

We learned that the couple had started their business over 20 years ago. Just after opening, they had hired a young lady just out of high school to do their bookkeeping. The young lady had stayed with them over the 20 years and over time had accumulated more and more financial responsibilities, including access to the couple's personal bank accounts, as well as bank accounts of other ventures the couple owned. In return for her loyalty, the woman was paid well, with good benefits, including paid vacations.

It was during a time that the bookkeeper was on vacation that the checks started to bounce, resulting in the bank calling the husband to let him know that the account was overdrawn. With their bookkeeper away, the couple had no one to answer their questions. While they tried to review and understand their bank statements, there were simply too many transactions in the accounts for them to gain an understanding of what had happened.

During our initial meeting, we asked the couple all about the bookkeeper and the various bank accounts she controlled. We also asked them if they thought the woman could have stolen funds from the accounts. Both husband and wife were adamant that there was no way the woman had stolen any money. We thought perhaps that is what the couple wanted the result to be, but based on our experience, we strongly suspected that the bookkeeper had been stealing their funds.

It did not take very long for us to see that the woman was using their funds for personal use. Funds were being transferred out of their accounts and into the woman's bank account, the same bank account where her direct deposit was routed. We updated counsel about our initial findings and recommended that the woman be placed on immediate administrative leave pending the outcome of our investigation. We also recommended that her email be suspended, along with her remote access to their systems, and that the keys and alarm codes be changed that day.

I still remember the couple's indifferent reaction. They said they were not going to undertake any of our recommendations. They maintained that if the woman had stolen from them, she must have had a good reason. Perhaps she needed the funds for some legitimate reason. They asked their attorney if they had to proceed with the investigation, or if they could simply add additional funds into their accounts to restore the balances and clear the checks. The attorney had the same reaction I did. He could not believe what he was hearing. What didn't we know about this situation? Why would the owners want the woman to continue working for them as if nothing happened even after knowing she had stolen a significant amount of their money? It made no sense. However, the couple continued the meeting as if everything was normal.

We asked the husband and wife why they weren't angry about what they'd learned. They told us there was no reason to get angry; it wasn't as if the woman was going to repay them the money, because she didn't have any. In addition, the woman had become so instrumental in their business and personal lives that they couldn't imagine having to start from scratch with someone new.

Their attorney advised them to get a better understanding of all the things this woman may have done, and he suggested that we continue our investigation, which we did. However, the woman was not placed on leave but was asked by the owners not to come to the office. During the investigation, they brought her work to her house and allowed her to continue working on projects. I will never understand why. The only explanation I can come up with is that the woman must have known some information about the couple or their businesses that they feared would come out if she was held accountable. Therefore, they were willing to continue business as usual rather than risk the release of compromising information.

In the end, we determined that the bookkeeper had diverted several hundred thousand dollars from the couple's businesses and personal bank accounts over the span of several years. We never found the starting point, but the oldest records we were provided contained evidence that she had been stealing their funds. As far as I know, she was never fired, prosecuted, or held accountable. She continued working for them after our involvement and may still be working there today, managing all of their financial affairs. ▨

When it comes to indifference, I've learned to be cautious of any individual who sits in a meeting and remains quiet and emotionless. While this is not likely to occur in a small meeting such as an interview, it does occur in larger meetings. I am cautious because I don't know what the individual is thinking, and I don't know how their behavior may change, with or without any notice.

First responders have a phrase that I live by, both on emergency calls and on fraud engagements: "Plan for the worst, and hope for the best." As I watch someone sitting quiet and impassive during a meeting, I wonder what might be going through their head. Are they about to burst with anger and hostility, like a storm that is off-radar but quietly brewing? Or are they about to break down and cry? Perhaps they don't understand what is happening. Or maybe their mind is in some faraway location, sitting on a beach under the hot sun, looking out over turquoise waters. I try to look for visual clues in their facial expression, body language, and posture. I watch their hands and check to see if they have brought anything with them to the meeting, such as a bag or briefcase.

I am especially alarmed when I know the individual has a history of being very emotional, yet during this meeting they are stoic.

After a while, I ask the individual if they have any questions or need anything clarified. I do this simply to get them to react so I can gauge their mental state. This strategy also allows me to make sure they're still participating in the meeting. I can remember a few meetings where I used this strategy and my question opened Pandora's Box, meaning once they started talking, they went on and on about things that may or may not have had anything to do with why we were meeting, and in some cases it was difficult to get them to focus on the issues at hand. I firmly believe that it is better to discover and address what is going on with the indifferent individual than to ignore it and wait to see what happens. Sometimes the individual is sitting on hidden emotions, but other times, the individual may simply be depressed.

 DEPRESSION

According to the Mayo Clinic, depression is "a mood disorder that causes a persistent feeling of sadness and loss of interest."[1] Signs and symptoms of depression vary and can include irritability, loss of interest, tiredness, and restlessness, as well as:

- Feelings of sadness, tearfulness, emptiness, or hopelessness
- Angry outbursts, irritability, or frustration, even over small matters
- Loss of interest or pleasure in most or all normal activities, such as sex, hobbies, or sports
- Sleep disturbances, including insomnia or sleeping too much
- Tiredness and lack of energy, so even small tasks take extra effort
- Reduced appetite and weight loss, or increased cravings for food and weight gain
- Anxiety, agitation, or restlessness
- Slowed thinking, speaking, or body movements
- Feelings of worthlessness or guilt, fixating on past failures or self-blame
- Trouble thinking, concentrating, making decisions, and remembering things
- Frequent or recurrent thoughts of death, suicidal thoughts, suicide attempts, or suicide
- Unexplained physical problems, such as back pain or headaches

Fraud examiners should expect to encounter individuals suffering from depression. In my experience, depression is especially common in elderly individuals who have fallen victim to some type of fraud scheme. It's also a common occurrence in parents in family matters where their children are involved in some type of dispute. I have felt depression myself in a personal matter that I was not professionally involved in.

The family I'd grown up with since childhood included three children, a daughter and two sons – just like my own family. I attended the same schools as these children, and the family's two sons are still among my closest friends.

Sadly, their father passed away suddenly when the children were in high school, and they continued to live on and off with their mother until adulthood and beyond. Most of my favorite memories involved doing something with these siblings, and the brothers were very close. I still refer to them as Butch Cassidy and the Sundance Kid.

A few years ago their mother passed away, and a falling out occurred between the three children. At one point, none of the siblings were speaking to each other, and the two brothers' relationship had strained to the breaking point. I continued interacting with each of them individually and listened as each talked about the other. The two brothers had been great friends, but they were two very different people. During that time, I learned more about each of them than I had growing up with them. I was truly sad to see them no longer talking to each other.

The division in the family stemmed from their sister's handling of their mother's affairs, a task that she'd done for many years, without sharing any information with her brothers. When records disappeared from their mother's house after she passed away, accusations and resentment abounded. Because I knew all three siblings and could be an independent and objective source of advice, I offered to intervene to seek a possible resolution. I agreed to review the financial records and obtain answers to the brothers' questions about their sister. I completed the review, provided reports to all three siblings, and ultimately helped them resolve their financial issues. However, other aspects of their conflict remained unresolved, and sadly a permanent division was created between the sister and her older brother. I thought the brothers would find a way to make amends and return to their former relationship, but sadly, I was mistaken. Each continued to talk with me independently, but neither had any desire to connect with the other. I thought about this rift all the time, and it made me sad each time I spoke with either of them.

I decided I needed to do something to fix the issue, so I set up a meeting, somewhere public for all three of us to have a beer and talk and laugh about old times. They agreed, but only because I had asked them each as a favor to meet with me. As expected, the meeting was a bit awkward at first, but before long we were laughing and reminiscing. Then we left for the night.

I knew one meeting alone would not help repair their relationship, so I set up another, and then another. On one occasion, I knew they were both at the agreed location waiting for me, so I called and told them something had come up and that I wouldn't be able to make it. I wanted them to interact without me, to see how it went.

After that, whenever I talked with one of the brothers, I would ask about the other one and learn they had just met for dinner or had a beer. Seeing them back together, in close to the same relationship as they'd previously had, has been one of my greatest accomplishments. It took a good six to nine months to repair their relationship. They may never know how happy it makes me to see them back together again. ▪

Although not an official task of a fraud engagement, the fraud examiner may be in a unique position to help a client work through an issue, like the brothers who no longer spoke with one another. Simply raising the issue and recommending that they start a dialog and try to find a way back to a relationship would be a great start. It would be unrealistic to think a fraud examiner's job extends to repairing relationships, but what I am recommending is that if the opportunity presents itself, see if there is anything you can do to help start the healing process. For me, getting the two brothers back together was more worthwhile and gratifying than solving their financial issues with their sister.

As a fraud examiner, you may find yourself in a unique position to provide objectivity and advice, not only within official fraud engagements, but also in any instance where you can draw upon experience to help resolve a matter.

When you think about what matters most in life, things like family, friends, companionship, health, and financial stability come to mind. When something happens to negatively impact any of these elements, an individual may become depressed. For example, if an individual invests his money with a friend who has promised that the venture will pay hefty dividends only to learn that the entire story was a ruse and their friend has stolen their life savings, that individual may become depressed. They may feel violated and stupid for having made such a decision.

In a business setting, if a business owner learns that his controller has stolen the company's funds, so that the owner cannot now pay his employees, vendors, and loans, he may become depressed. Everything he has worked for his entire life has been invested into his business, and he has now lost it all. Arresting the controller and filing a lawsuit will not likely recover the funds, and as a result the business may not survive for very long.

Suspects as well as victims will experience depression. For example, if a finance manager is found to have been stealing funds from her employer, she will now face termination. During her interview, the finance manager will be presented with the evidence and told that an insurance claim and a police matter are about to be initiated. The finance manager will be asked if she has any ability to repay the funds, which she most likely does not, since she has used that money to satisfy personal obligations. The finance manager now realizes that her spouse and family will find out what she's done, and she may face further consequences when that information comes out, such as her husband divorcing her. All these factors can lead to the suspect's experiencing depression.

In these instances, the fraud examiner's showing empathy is very powerful when working with these individuals, understanding how they would feel given the situation. There is a difference between sympathy and empathy, and I discuss this in a later chapter. During these meetings and interactions, I recommend you talk to the individual and ask them if they have any support structures in place. Do they have someone they can talk to, to help them work through their issues? An attorney may be able to help them with the legal aspects of their matter, but for all the other aspects, they will need someone who can console and emotionally support them.

Because of my unique background as a volunteer medic, I raise these issues during my meetings just as I would on an emergency medical call. It's important to recognize the humanity of the individuals in your cases and to treat them with respect and compassion.

When I have been working weekend nights on the ambulance, I've responded to many calls where elderly individuals who lived alone activated their emergency button so we would respond to their residence. Upon arrival, we find a perfectly healthy but lonely individual who just wants someone to talk to. Almost all of these calls happen in the middle of the night. Once we are on the scene, we have to decide whether to clear the call and leave or to stay for a short while. Unless we get another call, we generally stay and talk to the individual for a while. In other words, we choose to care. There are many lonely people out there in our communities, and most just want someone to talk to and care about them.

That was certainly the case in the following fraud matter I was involved in.

We were contacted by an attorney representing the daughter of a woman who had likely been the victim of a financial scheme. The mother had recently contacted her daughter in very distraught state. The mother had visited her investment advisor for morning coffee, as she had done many times in the past, but when she arrived, her advisor was not there. The mother thought something terrible must have happened to her advisor, and she wanted to contact the authorities and other resources to help find her.

Once the daughter calmed her mother down, she asked her mother to explain the situation in a little more detail. The mother explained that she had met this advisor less than a year ago at a coffee shop where they'd started talking. The next time they ran into each other, the advisor told the woman that she should come by her house some time for coffee. The mother took her up on her invitation and met her at her house. The next week she met the advisor at her house again. The mother said they talked about their families and their children. Eventually, they started sharing coffee on a weekly basis.

At one point, the advisor explained what she did for a living. She managed other people's funds, helping them understand different financial products. The advisor told her friend that she had left a firm after several years and decided to start her own firm so that she could offer services on a much more personal level. The mother described the advisor as sweet and never pushy. At one point, the mother asked the advisor for some financial advice, and she eventually opened an investment account with the advisor's firm. Over time, she'd transferred more and more of her savings over to the advisor, and the advisor would show her the results on colorful graphs while they shared coffee on her porch. The mother said this situation continued for months.

Then, one day, when they'd arranged to meet for coffee as usual, the mother arrived at the advisor's house only to find it empty. She was scared that something terrible had happened to her friend. Perhaps she had been abducted. The mother was panicking.

Before meeting with the attorney, the woman, and her daughter, we performed some research into this advisor, as well as into the address where the mother had met her for coffee. We discovered that the advisor's house had been rented and was now vacant and available for rent again. We learned that there was no licensed financial advisor with her name in the state, and we found nothing about her through searches and social media queries. We'd already suspected this was a scam perpetrated on an elderly woman with funds, and everything we found – or didn't find – seemed to support our theory.

When we met with the attorney, the woman, and her daughter, we asked the woman to bring the colorful graphs and charts that the advisor had provided her, so we could review them. As we had expected, the graphs showed no named financial institutions or account numbers. We surmised that the advisor had simply taken the woman's funds for her own use. When she had obtained all of the woman's life savings, the advisor had fled in the middle of the night.

We recommended that the matter be referred to local law enforcement to initiate a criminal investigation, since law enforcement had the best chance of identifying and locating the woman pretending to be a financial advisor.

However, we now had to break the sad news to the mother that her life savings were gone and that she had been the victim of a financial scheme. I remember that this conversation was very difficult, because the mother insisted we must be wrong, that something terrible must have happened to the advisor. All three of us talked to her, slowly explaining the scheme and what had happened to her funds. I remember the blank stare on the mother's face as she listened in disbelief. Her only concern was for the safety and well-being of her friend, the advisor.

She sat and pondered what she was going to do next now that she had no one to have coffee with. She couldn't process that most, if not all, of what the advisor had shared with her on a personal level had likely been made up – it had just been part of the scheme to befriend her so that she could steal her money. The mother said that having a new friend to have coffee with on a regular basis had kept her feeling alive and made it worthwhile to wake up in the morning. She was so excited every time she knew they were going to meet. She asked us what she would do now that her friend was gone. It was very sad. ▧

What is terrible is that this woman's case was not unique; these schemes are actually quite common. However, this was the only case I can remember where the client's depression made such an impression on me. I can still remember how this woman looked when she learned her new friend was gone forever. I am not entirely sure she ever really processed what actually happened.

DESPAIR

In an engagement, depression can easily lead to despair. If someone feels cornered and that there is no good way for them to escape, they can become desperate.

To better understand desperation, let's first look at something called the "fraud triangle." In the fraud field, the fraud triangle, developed from the works of Donald Cressey, identifies the factors or conditions that, if present, can cause an individual to commit fraud.[2] The three points of the fraud triangle are *perceived opportunity, rationalization*, and *perceived financial need*.

Perceived opportunity occurs when an individual has access to something that can be diverted for their personal gain or use, such as money or other assets. If a company or individual wants to minimize the risk of fraud, then they need to identify these perceived opportunities and make sure they have proper measures in place to prevent or detect any theft or misuse.

Rationalization is a mindset, an individual's ability to reframe their thefts as something other than stealing or fraud, such as "borrowing" with the goal of paying back. However, the individual's "borrowing" is done without the permission or knowledge of the rightful owner.

Perceived financial need, the last corner of the triangle, is the individual's reasoning for diverting funds or other assets to which they have access. Often, people who would otherwise not steal from their employer end up in a personal financial situation that they believe can't be solved using their available funds and resources. If they have access to funds that could solve their issue and they can rationalize that they are not *actually* stealing, then they are likely to divert the funds. This problem often snowballs when the individual's needs outweigh the initial solution, and the individual once again "borrows" funds. Eventually, the scheme becomes large and increasingly hard to control.

Many individuals accused of stealing blame their actions on acts of desperation, such as trying to prevent the bank from foreclosing on their mortgage. In some of the cases I've investigated, the individual turned to stealing only when things happened in their personal life that were beyond their control. I can remember several cases where the individual's spouse left and filed for divorce, leaving the individual to provide for children and pay all the costs associated with maintaining the household. Divorce courts are designed to help spouses in these situations, but the delay and backlog in family courts easily prolongs the process for months or longer. In the meantime, the remaining spouse is responsible for the mortgage, utilities, food, transportation, insurance, taxes, and other living expenses. If the spouse who left was the higher earner, it is likely that the remaining spouse will not be able to sustain the status quo for very long. I trust any fraud examiner can appreciate how situations like this can occur and how good people might make bad decisions when acting out of desperation.

Desperation also comes into play in cases where the individual accused of a crime first realizes the potential consequences they face – for example, incarceration or losing custody of their children. Individuals in these situations may plead with the fraud examiner not to get the police involved. I can remember many of these interviews and the strength of the individuals' desperation. These are difficult encounters. As much as you want to have compassion for the individual, you also have to remember that the investigation needs to be completed. I use empathy in my interactions and maintain an objective, non-judgmental tone when meeting with the individual. I am aware of the potential consequences they may face, and I don't try to minimize them. I simply tell them I understand how someone could feel in their situation, and ask them how we can work together to get all of the facts on the table. I tell them that the sooner the details are known, the sooner the case can be resolved.

While suspects often become desperate, this emotion is common to victims as well. I have encountered business owners who, once they learned that a significant amount of funds had been diverted from their business, became despondent. Once the shock of the news settled in, the owner realized their business would not have sufficient funds to cover upcoming payroll. I've watched as the owner started to process the domino effect this would cause. With no funds to make payroll, he would not be able to pay his employees. If he did not pay his employees, then each employee's household would be negatively impacted. And so on . . .

I have seen cases where the business could not survive after a significant theft and had to close its doors. Employees lost their jobs, and creditors sued to get paid, resulting in the owner's filing for bankruptcy. You can easily see how a successful business owner who is now facing unexpected bankruptcy can tip into despair.

In these cases, I try to never end a meeting with someone experiencing despair. I have seen too many cases where tragic and irreversible things occurred after an individual fell into despair. Individuals who can see no happy future or outcome their this situation start to think about suicide as a solution.

In these types of situations, I try to look for the light at the end of the tunnel. I attempt to get the individual to focus on positive things and potential solutions. There is often a way to fix these situations, but someone needs to work with the individual to help them find possible solutions and navigate their way out of their problems. Someone needs to care. I have yet to read any fraud examination manual that mentions this fact, but it's true. Someone needs to care about the humans involved in these cases.

I have worked with many victims, even after a fraud engagement was complete, to help them find ways to continue on and thrive. I did not do anything extraordinary; all I did was care about their well-being. In some cases, I talked to the person on a daily basis, and in others I made myself available as needed. I don't consider the time I spend listening to these people and providing them with advice to be billable hours. Rather, it is a return on their investment.

I have developed great relationships through these efforts, with individuals I now call friends. These people text me on my birthday and on holidays. Some have expressed their gratitude more than others, but I trust each one has appreciated the time I invested in them and their businesses.

The following case always comes to mind as one of the most appreciative clients I have had in 30 years.

We were referred to a local business owner who was going through some litigation with his siblings. Since the business was located not far from where I'd grown up, I knew of the company and what they did. At one point in my childhood, my family had been a customer of theirs, and I remember making many trips to the business with my parents. Going into this new matter, I knew the business had been around for a long time, but I didn't know the owner or anyone who worked there.

We spoke with the owner and learned more about why he needed our services. The business had originated with the owner's father, who over time had passed the business along to his son. His son, the current owner, had worked in the business his entire life, while his brothers had not. The owner described working long hours and sometimes spending seven days a week trying to keep up with the business's volume, all the while earning a modest compensation. He told us that when his father passed away, the trouble with his brothers started. All three sons had been named beneficiaries in their father's estate, and his brothers believed they'd received less than they were entitled due to the undue influence that their brother, the current owner, had over their father. The owner showed us the obligations that he'd signed to his father when he bought the business and related properties. He said he had financial records to show he had been making the payments to his father on those notes.

Both of his brothers lived in other states, and each had decided years earlier that they wanted nothing to do with their father's business. Now that they had received distributions from their father's estate, they wanted to scrutinize all of the activity that had occurred between their father and brother, going back many years. The owner had been working with attorneys to resolve the issues and settle his father's estate. To date, he had been unsuccessful in finding any resolution with his brothers.

The owner had an outside accountant who his father had used, and recently he'd hired a new bookkeeper recommended by his accountant. The owner told us he had no faith in the new bookkeeper and that his records were a mess. He said his life was a mess, and that in addition to running the business and the properties, trying to resolve the issues with his brothers had pushed him to the edge emotionally.

We started working with him, reviewing financial documents as far back as when he had first signed the obligations purchasing the business and properties from his father. We reviewed the business's tax returns and became intimate with the business records. We also reviewed the estate's finances, the father's will, two trust documents established with the father's will, and many more records. We then set up a time to meet with the new bookkeeper.

Before we had a chance to meet with the new bookkeeper, the owner called to tell us he believed this bookkeeper was stealing from the business. Although he had brought her on as an outside consultant, she had put herself on payroll and enrolled in the company's group health insurance. The owner had also found evidence that she was doing other inappropriate things. He'd called his accountant to find out more about her and learned she was the accountant's fiancée, something the accountant had failed to disclose when he brought her on. The owner threw his hands up and called us to seek our advice. We set up a meeting for later that day and told him he needed to terminate the bookkeeper immediately. (We never met the bookkeeper, since she was fired after our call and told never to return.)

During the meeting, the owner told us he had pretty much given up. He was still getting over his father's passing; he was fighting with his brothers, with whom he'd had no real relationship within the past 20 years; and he'd hired who he'd thought were the right people to help him, only to learn they were thieves. He was just tired of everything that was happening. We could see he was physically and emotionally spent.

That night, we started developing a plan, listing out all the things that needed to happen in order to get the owner resolution and for him to get his life back on track. We started by firing the accountant and bringing closure to the bookkeeper issue. We provided him with the name of a new accountant, a colleague and trusted advisor of ours, and we sent off an introductory email to set up an initial meeting.

We then called a bookkeeper colleague and arranged for her to take over the bookkeeping functions for the owner's business and properties.

Having worked with her for years, we knew, liked, and trusted her. She was a self-starter who could come in and clean house.

Then we went into the owner's business office, one of the biggest messes we had ever seen, and decided we would return the next day to clean out, disinfect, and organize the office before the new bookkeeper started. We called the owner's attorney, provided an update, and explained our plan. On the list of items to complete were resolving the estate and resolving trust issues with his brothers. We told the attorney that we wanted to set up a meeting to determine where things stood from a legal perspective and to identify what we needed to get the issues resolved. During that call, we set up the meeting.

I then provided the owner with my cell phone number and told him to call me anytime to discuss anything that was on his mind. By the end of the next day, his office was clean and organized and the business's records were boxed, labeled, and moved into storage. A start date was in place for the new bookkeeper, who would meet us at the business on her first day. A meeting was also scheduled with the new accountant.

Over the next six months, we worked with the owner on every issue that came up in his case. Since he was uncomfortable dealing with the old accountant, we acted as his intermediary, including writing the termination of services letter and retrieving his records from the accountant's firm. I should note that the accountant was not pleasant to deal with, but we made it happen anyway.

In a relatively short period of time, we helped stabilize his business and resolve some of the issues wreaking havoc in his life. We referred the owner to a new business attorney in town and helped him put things into place, such as leases for the various properties, that should have been in existence for years.

Within a year, his legal matters were settled, final payments had been made to the brothers, and the owner finally had closure on those longstanding issues. We told him to close the book on this time in his life, put it up on a shelf, and never revisit it. The owner still uses the book analogy with me to this day.

During the engagement, we developed a friendship with the owner that continues to this day. My firm, unlike most accounting firms, does not have traditional clients. We are project-oriented, so we are retained on a specific matter, and when it is resolved, we move onto the next matter. Thus, we have no recurring clients. The owner of this business is the closest we have to a traditional client, in that we remain in contact with him regularly to ensure that things are still going well for him and to provide him with a sounding board when he needs to make big (or little) decisions. A text message from this owner is usually the first communication I receive on my birthday and on holidays, and we have a reminder set in my firm's systems to send him a birthday card every year. ▪

The magic recipe to helping him get all of his issues resolved? **I cared**.

 INTOXICATION

There is a strong relationship between depressed and desperate individuals and substance abuse. While I am not an expert in these fields, I have seen the relationship time and again on emergency medical calls, where I have been working on the ambulance. Sadly, many of them resulted in overdoses and the person's death.

Although intoxication and substance abuse are not emotions, they often result from an emotional state or event, and so they are worth mentioning here. As I began writing this book, I recognized that no training had prepared me for so many of the situations I encountered on fraud engagements. Starting out, I had an accounting education, limited work experience, and little in the way of an investigative background. When it came to difficult human interactions, I had virtually no training. However, as I gained experience in my field, less and less surprised me on these cases. Much of what I know today I attribute to my previous engagements and experiences, which were an education in and of themselves.

I can honestly state I never expected to interact with individuals under the influence of alcohol or drugs as part of a fraud engagement. When I worked on the ambulance, I certainly expected this situation to occur. I have had many interactions with intoxicated and addicted people in the context of emergency medicine. I presumed, however, that when I worked on fraud engagements, interviewing bookkeepers, controllers, chief financial officers (CFOs), and others, I would not encounter the same types of issues.

My eyes were opened when I first interacted with an intoxicated individual on a matter. Early in the meeting, I recognized that the individual was under the influence, so I chose to postpone the interaction until I could develop a strategy or reschedule with the hope that the individual would be sober the next time. In that particular case, there was no second interaction, so there was no opportunity to execute our new strategy.

What I've learned working on the ambulance is that individuals under the influence of alcohol and/or drugs can be unpredictable and dangerous. The typical fraud examiner is not trained or prepared to deal with these scenarios, and so my advice is: When you encounter someone who appears to be intoxicated, end the interaction and reschedule to a later date, perhaps when you can have additional resources present. As I have mentioned before, your personal safety is paramount.

It's also important to stay alert to the possibility of intoxication throughout an engagement. Sometimes you may be having an interaction with a sober individual, only to have things change later in the meeting. For instance, if a meeting is not going well and the client takes a break, they might access alcohol or drugs during this time and then return to the meeting under the influence. This happened in a case we handled. As soon as we noted the individual's intoxication, we ended the meeting and left the premises.

We were engaged by an attorney representing a condominium association. The owners had retained the attorney because the property manager, who was an owner of several units and also resided in the complex, kept all of the association's financial affairs secret. The property manager handled all of the common fee collections, made the deposits, incurred the costs, paid the bills, funded the reserves, and ensured that all the bookkeeping was up to date. The issue the owners had was that the manager would not share any of the association's financial information with the other owners, even though the articles of incorporation and bylaws allowed all owners equal access to the finances.

Month after month, the attorney tried to get the property manager to provide access to the books and records. When none was provided, he initiated a lawsuit against the property manager on behalf of the owners.

The attorney filed a motion to require the property manager to provide access, and the judge granted the motion. The property manager now had to provide the records or be held in contempt of the court order.

We contacted the property manager and set a time to meet with her in her office, which was located in one of the units in the association. We asked her to have all of the association's accounting, books, records, and bank statements ready for us when we arrived so that we could review them. Prior to the meeting, we performed a background investigation on the property manager and learned that she had been convicted of embezzlement in the past. We also learned that she maintained a few limited liability companies (LLCs).

On the scheduled date, we arrived at her unit. After brief introductions, she led us into a dining room. There were no records out for our review (which is not uncommon in these cases). We asked her for the records, and she said she would have to get them for us. We waited while she walked from room to room. After a while, she brought us the bank statements. She stated that they were her only copies and that we would need to review them in her unit, as she would not let the statements or any other information leave the premises. We asked her if she had a copier that we could use, and she said no.

What she didn't anticipate was that we had come to the meeting prepared. In one of our bags, we had a portable scanner, which allowed us to scan to PDFs any records she provided. As we set it up, we could tell she was surprised that we were prepared to copy her records.

All morning long, we asked her for records, and she provided them to us piecemeal. Rather than spending time reviewing them in her unit, we focused on scanning them, as they might disappear after the day's meeting (another common occurrence in these engagements). We could see her watching us from her kitchen, and we glimpsed her in a mirror watching us from other parts of the unit. She seemed to be getting increasingly stressed.

Once the scanning was nearly complete, we started looking at the documents. We could see transactions between the association and the LLCs that we had identified as her entities. We also noted personal expenses paid on an association credit card.

Conscious that lunchtime was approaching, we called the woman into the room, asked her to sit down, and started asking her questions about the association. Her responses were short and vague. We selected a few transactions with her LLCs and asked her to explain the details of each. From what we could decipher from the statements, each appeared to be simply a transfer of funds into one of her LLCs. The woman said she would provide us the details for each of the transactions. We also asked her about a few of the personal charges on the credit card. She explained that she had receipts for every purchase and that she would have to get them for us to review. She asked us how long we planned to be at her unit, and we indicated that we could stay all day to complete the procedures. She asked if we could break for lunch so that while we were away she could gather the additional information for us to review.

We typically do not stop for lunch, but since she asked us to give her time, we packed up our scanner and laptops and left for lunch. Sadly, we had to leave all of the association's records behind, per her instructions.

When we returned, the door to the unit was open and she called down for us to come in. We could see her standing in the kitchen, and it appeared that the files were as we left them on the table. It did not appear that she had added any new information to the table. We asked her to join us, and when she came into the room, we could tell right away that she had been been drinking during our absence. Her walk had altered, her eyes were glazed over, and her speech was slurred. I easily identified the smell of alcohol on her. We asked her how her lunch had been, and she said it had been fine. We then asked her if she had located the records for us. She said she had already provided them to us before lunch. We reminded her that she'd asked us to leave for lunch because she needed time to gather additional records. She said we must have misunderstood what she said, because all of the association's records were on the table.

Knowing that the rest of the day would be pointless, we decided to leave. We had already scanned all of the records on the table, and staying in the unit while she was intoxicated could create other issues for us based on the unpredictable behavior of intoxicated individuals. ■

To complete the story of that case, back at our office we were able to use the scanned records to identify all the transactions that involved the property manager's LLCs, as well as all of the personal charges made on the association's credit card. We provided counsel with an update as to what happened, along with a schedule of the identified activity. We never interacted with the property manager again, nor did we need to, as we had all of her records.

Not all fraud examiners have training and experience dealing with intoxication or individuals under the influence of substances. Some fraud examiners will have experience through other contexts, such as being a first responder, as is my case. However, even with experience, when working in the role of a fraud examiner, one will not have the resources that would otherwise be available as a first responder. Interactions with these individuals can often be unpredictable and potentially violent. The most important takeaway from this discussion is for the fraud examiner to recognize when someone is potentially intoxicated or under the influence of substances, and to realize that whatever was planned for that interaction, your safety is paramount and that you need to leave that situation and identify another time and place to reschedule.

SAFEGUARDING YOUR CASE

As I was writing this story, I recalled another short story worth sharing about trusting clients.

I went to the home office of a woman who owned an LLC along with her husband. The woman was the primary recordkeeper for the business, and when she and her husband decided to divorce, she'd locked her husband out of their business and denied him access to the financial information. By court order, I had been provided access to the records, and in this instance, I was able to use the photocopier in her office to copy key records. The woman was very pleasant and very talkative. She wanted to know about my background and family. I had no need to build a rapport with her – I simply needed access to copy the records – so I kept conversation to a minimum. She wanted to know if I had found anything and what I was looking for in their books and records. Again, I kept my responses to a bare minimum and just focused on making the copies.

When I had finished, I put all the copies into my bags and prepared to leave. Noting the distance I would be driving back to my office, I asked to use her bathroom. She happily showed me the way. When I returned, my things were just as I left them. I thanked her for her help and departed. I then drove to my office and secured the files for the night. The next day, when I started reviewing the copies, I noticed right away that things I remembered seeing and copying yesterday were not there. I put all of the copies on our conference room table and searched for the missing items. They weren't there. That was when it dawned on me that, while I had been in the bathroom at the woman's office, the woman had gone into my bags and taken certain copies out.

I considered this a rookie mistake. That very day, I ordered bags that locked, and from that day forward, I always used those bags and never let records out of my sight. In hindsight, I had never had someone access and take my files, so I hadn't been on alert to the possibility. However, I should never have left those records unaccompanied and unlocked. Lesson learned – never again. ▓

I share this story because the fraud examiner, too, can be subjected to manipulation through the use of emotions. I trust anyone with experience in this field will recall at least one instance if not many. In this case the woman was extremely nice to me, showed a genuine interest in our brief discussions, was very accommodating, and appeared genuine and trustworthy. It caused me to lower my guard, something that has not happened since then.

Learn from my experience. While on an engagement, never leave your computer and files unattended during breaks. Always pack them up and bring them with you, or leave someone on the team with them to watch over them.

A bit of warning as I proceed to the subject of the following chapter. As I mentioned earlier, individuals who are stressed, depressed, and desperate sometimes turn to suicide as a solution to their situation. Tragically, this happens in fraud engagements. I apologize in advance for the heavy discussion, but a book discussing client emotions would be incomplete without discussing the potential for suicide.

 END NOTES

1. "Depression (major depressive disorder)," Mayo Clinic, February 3, 2018, accessed January 11, 2021, https://www.mayoclinic.org/diseases-conditions/depression/symptoms-causes/syc-20356007.
2. Donald R. Cressey, *Other People's Money* (Montclair, NJ: Patterson Smith, 1973), p. 30.

CHAPTER SEVEN

Suicide

WHEN I STARTED IN this field over 30 years ago, I never thought I'd encounter homicides, suicides, and other violent crimes in the context of fraud examinations. Perhaps I was a bit naive, but I thought fraud investigations involved bookkeeping records, bank statements, canceled checks, deposit records, financial reports, and payroll registers. Those are the things we'd learned about in my accounting classes. I anticipated investigating tax fraud or employee theft, but never imagined that as an accountant I would be consulted on a multiple-victim homicide. In hindsight, I underestimated the value of my criminal justice degree in this field.

As a young adult, I had participated in a police explorer program for seven years, starting when I was 14 and continuing right through high school and college. As a part of this program, I rode around in police cars and so was aware of violent crimes. I just never expected to confront them later in my career in the context of fraud and white-collar crime.

I remember once listening to a speaker at a fraud conference talk about a case he'd worked on, where as he'd closed in on the individual he believed had committed the fraud, the individual killed himself. That was the first time I made the connection between fraud and suicide. As I considered the amount of stress experienced by a person accused of committing fraud, I realized that such reactions might not be uncommon. During a fraud engagement, depression and despair are common emotional states that can lead to someone taking their own life or the lives of others.

Just as no training exists for addressing client emotions during fraud engagements, no training exists that prepares fraud examiners to identify whether someone they are interacting with on an engagement is at risk of killing themselves. My background is unique in that I have 25 years of experience working on an ambulance and have attended classes and training sessions on the subject of suicide. Sadly, I have encountered far too many people on calls who were suicidal, along with others who accomplished their mission prior to our arrival.

However, a fraud examiner generally receives no training on what to do when the person they're meeting with tells them they are thinking of suicide or makes an off-the-cuff comment about suicide. If you happen to be the first person this individual has told about their desire or plan, you find yourself in a position of great responsibility. If you choose to do nothing, some of these clients will actually kill themselves.

My advice on this topic comes not from a legal position, but rather from a moral position. Of course, my background is different than most. As a first responder, emergency medical technician, and Boy Scout leader, I'm used to having legal duties in each role. If I witness abuse or other issues that could affect someone's health and safety, I am required to take action. In those contexts, if someone told me they were thinking of killing themselves or that they had tried to commit suicide, I would have a legal duty to get them help. In my home state of Connecticut, the law requires of first responders that if someone merely mentions suicidal ideations (i.e., expresses thoughts of suicide) to them, even if they later take it back or say they didn't really mean it, they are required to have them transported to a medical facility for evaluation. If the suicidal person goes willingly to the medical facility they can better control the length of time that they stay there. However, if they do not go willingly, then law enforcement is required to complete an emergency committal referral, and the individual can be held at the medical facility for up to 72 hours. The goal is to get the individual help so that they don't end up killing themselves.

Most fraud examiners do not share my background, training, and experience, and they likely have no training when it comes to dealing with suicidal individuals. Most fraud examiners are also likely under no legal requirement to act if they encounter someone with suicidal ideations. However, if you chose to do nothing in these circumstances and the person does end up committing suicide, you will still have to come to terms with how you handled the interaction.

I recognize that suicide is not an easy subject for most people to discuss, and I am by no means trying to pass judgment on others' actions in these circumstances. All I am saying is that based on your decision in each instance – and hopefully you will never encounter one – you will have to live with the outcome. And even if you do try to get an individual help, they may end up committing suicide anyway. In these circumstances, you will also have come to terms with what happened. I know I did.

Some time ago, my firm experienced a terrible year involving suicides related to our fraud engagements. I describe two of the matters in the following stories. However, my year also included two other non-work-related suicides and one suicidal ideation. Dealing with all of this in the course of one year was more than I could process. The hardest scenario for me to deal with involved a Boy Scout who was the age of my oldest son. He'd been in the troop for seven years with my son, and I knew him well. We had hiked, biked, camped, and canoed together. Both he and my son eventually became Eagle Scouts together. Although this boy had experienced some common issues that teenagers tend to do, he had overcome them and grown into a fine young man who was planning on attending college. However, on the night we were celebrating my firm's tenth anniversary, we received a call telling us that this boy had hung himself. I am still numb as I write this, and he passed away in 2015. I will never forget that experience.

A short time later, another Boy Scout asked to speak to me in private during one of our weekly meetings. He told me that he and his brother had come home from school in the afternoon to find that their mother's boyfriend had broken into their house and shot himself. At that point, the boyfriend still had a pulse, so the boy and his brothers performed CPR on him until help arrived. The boyfriend later died at the hospital. This boy's question to me was: Who could his family call to clean their house? I thought, "What a terrible question to have to ask." While the boy and his brothers told me they were okay, I knew that they were going to have issues down the road when they had had time to process what had happened.

Another case where I encountered suicide involved a family matter, where two brothers had accused their other brother of stealing from the family business. The two brothers had no active role in the business, but they believed their brother had been stealing money to sustain his lifestyle. Our client was the brother who was accused of stealing. We had met him a few times before the year-end holidays, and when he called me just before New Year's Eve, he was very distraught. I drove to meet him at his business, where I found him very upset. At times, he broke down crying. He told me he simply could not take it anymore. During our meeting, he said he should just kill himself. That would make all his issues go away.

I remember yelling at him. I wasn't trying to be mean; it was just that I had experienced too many individuals committing suicide that year, and I wasn't going to let it happen again. I told him I was going to get him help and that together we were going to work through the issues. I was not going to let him harm himself. I reminded him of his daughter and how she would feel if he killed himself. I knew from training and experience that seldom do people thinking of suicide consider the lifelong impact their suicide will have on family and friends.

I made a decision right then and there to prevent this man from hurting himself. I stayed with him and talked to him for a long while, then I made sure he had all my contact information. I told him to reach out to me 24/7 for anything, that I would be there for him. I made sure he went to his mother's house that night, and I called him first thing the next morning. Every day for several weeks, I either called him or sent him texts. I liked this client, and although he had more issues than any one person should have to deal with, he simply needed someone to help him resolve them. I knew that once his issues were addressed, he would be in a better spot, if for no other reason than he knew that someone cared about his situation. This individual did not end up committing suicide. I still talk to him all the time.

I know from training and experience that many individuals who mention suicide are crying out for help – they don't actually want to kill themselves. Instead, they want someone to help them and care about them. When it comes to suicidal ideations, remember that if you choose not to do anything in response, the individual may go through with their plans. To my mind, no fraud scheme is worth killing yourself over. The consequences of committing fraud can at times be severe, but nothing is worth killing yourself over.

In sharing these experiences, I am not suggesting that you become the best friend of everyone you encounter who has suicidal ideations. In my work as a medic, I have encountered many suicidal patients, and I simply got them to a medical facility so that they could get help. Each instance will be unique.

My hope is that you never have to deal with this issue, but by reading about some situations I've encountered, at least you will be aware that a similar situation could arise on one of your cases. The following case is one that was hard for us because we knew suicide was likely to happen, and we told the attorneys about it so that they would get the individual help and prevent it, and yet she still took her own life.

We received a call asking us to attend a meeting with two different attorneys to discuss a potential fraud matter. When we arrived, the attorneys told us they wanted to provide us with a brief background of the case prior to their mutual client arriving for the meeting. They said their client, a woman in her early sixties, held power of attorney over her father and managed all of his financial affairs. Her father was in declining health, and although their client had siblings, she was the closest to her father. She lived with him in a historic house in the city.

The attorneys told us the names of the client and her father and asked if we had done any work for them in the past. We had not, but we recognized their names from recent media coverage alleging that the daughter had misused her father's funds. The state was currently investigating the matter. The attorneys said that this meeting was the first opportunity they'd had to meet with their client, although they had previously spoken with her on the phone.

A short time later, their client arrived and joined our meeting. The attorneys introduced us and discussed how they knew her father. They told the woman we were meeting to help her straighten out the books and finances relating to her father's finances. They then asked her to explain in her own words what had happened.

The woman started her story back when she was growing up. She described how close she'd been with her father. Over the years, her siblings had gotten married and moved away, but she had never married. Instead, she'd stayed with her father. They had done everything together, and now that he was sick, she was able to take care of him at home. He had been in and out of the hospital a great deal and was presently back in the hospital. She said she didn't know if he would come home again. Then she started to cry.

After a few moments, she regained her composure and the attorneys asked her about her father's finances. She said she had records for everything, but that she wasn't the most organized person. The attorneys told her that that was what my firm had been hired for, to help her organize the records and address the allegations.

We asked her questions about the records, where they were maintained, and in what format. She said that all of the records were at their house, but not in the best order. We discussed going to her house to obtain, organize, and review the records, and we decided we would meet there tomorrow. During the meeting, the woman's sad expression and silent demeanor did not change. Periodically, she wiped tears from her eyes.

The next day, I brought one of my staff members with me to the woman's house. The woman answered the door and let us into the foyer. The house was in quite a state of disarray. To our left was a large office with a hospital bed in the middle of the room, which was far from clean. There were also boxes, stacks of papers, gadgets, and other items stacked along all of the walls. There was no sign of anyone else at home. The woman had the same sad, blank stare on her face and showed no emotions during our visit. We asked her if she had gone through any of the piles of papers to segregate financial information from everything else. She said she had not.

As we started looking through the piles in the office, we noticed a large locked file cabinet. We asked the woman if she knew what was in it, but she said she didn't. We then asked her if it was possible there were financial records in the cabinet. She said there might be. Since she didn't know where the key was, we eventually ended up prying the file cabinet open with a crowbar. Inside, we found no financial records, only medical records, family mementos, and photos. The woman flipped through the items, tears rolling down her face.

We spent a few hours going through the piles she had identified that could contain financial records, and we segregated them into boxes to be safeguarded at our office. We then carried the boxes to my car and provided the woman a receipt for the records. Finally, we asked her if there could be financial records anywhere else in the house. She led us through different areas of the house as she looked around for more records, but in the end she found none. As we left, we asked her how her father was doing. She said that he was dying and that he wasn't ever coming home. Tears ran down her face, and she said she needed to get to the hospital to see him. We thanked her for her help and left.

Based on my two meetings with the woman, my gut feeling was that she was going to be fine as long as her father was still alive but that when he passed away, she was probably going to kill herself. It seemed obvious to me that her father was everything to her, and without him, she believed she had nothing left to live for. We were concerned and called the attorneys to share our thoughts. We told them they needed to do something to get the woman help, because we firmly believed she was going to kill herself. They said they believed the same thing and agreed to try to get her help.

Over the next few weeks, we identified a bookkeeper who worked with the woman and maintained books and records of the father's finances. Based on the name and number our client provided, we were able to track down the bookkeeper. When we called her, a man answered and asked us why we wanted to speak to her. We told him we were working with our client to address the state's allegations. The man never allowed us to speak to the bookkeeper, but he did tell us we could retrieve a computer she used, since the father had paid for it. He said the bookkeeper had told him there were no other records and that the records were all with the daughter. We wondered why the bookkeeper wouldn't simply speak with us directly. Could she be hiding something?

We later received a message that a gentleman had left a computer at my firm's front desk. He did not provide his name, only the name of the father and daughter who employed the bookkeeper.

My hope was that the computer would provide explanations for many of the checks and transfers that the state had identified. The state did not have access to this computer, so we presumed that the state had obtained bank records and performed their own analysis. We called to ask our client about the bookkeeper and the computer. She said that the information we were seeking about her father's finances would be in there, as the bookkeeper kept track of everything. We were cautiously optimistic.

After preserving a copy of the computer's hard drive, we accessed the computer and the accounting software program. Much to our disappointment, the accounting records in the computer were a mess. When we compared the computer records to the actual bank statements, we found little that made any sense to us. Ideally, the two would have matched.

We called the attorneys and provided them with an update. We then called the woman and asked her why the bookkeeper's records were so different from the bank statements. She said she didn't know; the two should have agreed. The woman said she'd provided the bookkeeper with all the financial information on a regular basis. We asked the woman why she thought the bookkeeper wouldn't speak with us, but she said she didn't know. We then asked her if she thought the bookkeeper could be responsible for the transactions being investigated by the state. She said that the bookkeeper had full access and authority, so she could have.

Shortly after securing the bookkeeper's computer, we saw in the media that the woman's father had passed away. We also received word from the woman's attorneys, since they were planning on attending his funeral services. Once again, we raised our concern that the woman would kill herself. Once again, the attorneys said they understood and would address the issue.

I remember vividly what happened next. It was a Sunday night, and I was watching the late evening news in bed. There was a breaking news story: Emergency vehicles had been dispatched to a historic home in the city. There were no specifics, since the details of the event were still unfolding, but a news crew was en route to a certain address, and more information would be coming later in the newscast. Based on the address, I knew what had happened. The daughter had killed herself. I shut off the news. In the morning, when I checked back in with the news, my prediction was confirmed. Sadly, the woman had ended her own life. ■

A fraud examiner should also be prepared for the aftermath of a client suicide. In our case we were not prepared, but we also had little experience in this area. After her suicide, we had a unique issue to address with the woman's attorneys – what to do with all the records and the computer we had collected. The state no longer had someone to pursue, so their case would be closed. We then ended up transferring the records to the attorneys, who returned them to the family per their request. We called the number for the bookkeeper and informed her that the computer could be picked up from our office, which it was.

Her memory lives on. Periodically over the next year or so, I received random Facebook friend suggestions, identifying the client as a possible friend for me to connect with. Each time, it was an eerie reminder of a very sad woman who believed she had lost everything when she lost her father and had nothing left to live for. Very sad.

I still feel upset about the woman in this case. Her whole life had been centered around her father. When he passed, she must have felt there was no point in living. However, she still had family, and she was a beneficiary of his estate. She could have chosen to address the fraud allegations, and even if they were proven, she may not have suffered any consequences. Either way, she would have been surrounded by people who wanted to help her resolve her issues so she could grieve her father's passing and then get on with her life.

All the training you undergo as a fraud examiner may tell you not to get emotionally involved in matters, but that is easier said than done. Fraud examiners are still human. I discuss how to maintain your physical and emotional equilibrium in response to client emotions in a later chapter.

COFFEE-SHOP MEETING

In another case involving a client suicide, we only had one interaction with the individual, but he quickly became the prime target of our fraud investigation.

We met an attorney and his clients at a law firm within days of receiving their initial call. I sat and listened to the clients describe financial improprieties they'd recently discovered within their business. The clients were an owner of a gas station and convenience store and a woman who worked for him as a recordkeeper. The clients explained to me how their store manager had assembled register and system reports, reconciled the amounts to bank deposits and cash drawer balances, and maintained the information contemporaneously in daily bundles for each day, 365 days a year, for the past four years. They had samples of the daily bundles, which they shared with me to highlight the differences they had identified in the manager's reconciliations. In short, the owner and his assistant had been reviewing the daily bundles because the store's bank deposits had been diminishing without any explanation, and the monthly cash available within the business had declined to an alarming level. The owner stated that, up until the previous six months, the bank balances within the store's accounts had been sufficient. The minimal cash balances were a new problem. The owner had asked the manager what was happening at the store, but the manager had provided him with no explanation. The owner terminated the manager that day and took over managing the store.

The owner and his assistant had now identified shortages between the amounts sold per register reports and the amounts deposited into the bank account. After performing a quick trend analysis of the bank balances, the owner determined that in two years alone, the monthly deposits were down more than $100,000. As he spoke, he became very angry. He stood up and started banging his finger on the report he'd compiled. He said his manager had stolen from him, and he wanted him put in jail. He said he wanted his money back, and he wanted the manager to go to prison. Then he asked me if I could help him do this.

I told him I had questions, the first being how I could connect with his former manager to interview him. The owner asked me when I wanted to meet with him. I said as soon as possible. I asked the attorney if there was any reason why we couldn't call the former manager and set up a meeting. The attorney said there wasn't, so the owner called his former manager on his cell phone right then. When the former manager answered his phone, the owner told him that he'd hired a new accountant to help straighten out the store's books, and the accountant wanted to meet with him to understand how the daily bundles worked. The former manager agreed to meet, and I set off to meet with him at a local coffee shop about 30 minutes away. (The owner had mentioned at the meeting that his former manager had a concealed-carry pistol permit, so I wanted to meet him in a public place with plenty of customer traffic to minimize the risk that he would get angry and try to harm me.)

I arrived first at the coffee shop and bought a coffee. Shortly thereafter, the owner came in, along with a man in his mid- to late fifties. The owner introduced us, and the former manager sat down at my table. The owner said he was returning to his store, and he left us alone to talk. I told the former manager that I had been recently hired to understand and reconcile the store's records, and I needed his help. I proceeded to ask him about his background and his duties at the store. When he answered, he had an edge about him. When I asked him why he was reacting so defensively, he said he was "pissed off" that the owner had fired him and that he'd loved his job as manager. He said he'd done nothing wrong. One day the owner had simply come along, asked him why cash was down, and fired him. He said he'd given his life to the store for four years, working virtually every day without a vacation or break, and the reward he received was being terminated for no reason.

I told him I didn't know the details about what had led up to his termination. My job was just to straighten out the store's records so things could move forward. I told him that what had happened between him and the owner was beyond the scope of my job.

I then asked him about the other store employees and how the schedule and cash registers worked. He described four individuals who worked at the store at various times and how loose the store's internal controls and procedures were with regard to segregating employee transactions and activity. All the employees shared one or two system login names and the system was not reset in between employee shift changes. Thus, trying to segregate daily transactions and activity between each worker would be difficult, if not impossible.

I then asked him about the differences the owner had identified. He said he didn't know why there were differences. I asked him if he suspected any of his employees of stealing from the store. He said he'd tried investigating different issues that had occurred over time, but he'd never been able to reconcile the differences sufficiently to attach them to a specific individual. I asked him if he had ever discussed his concerns about these differences with the owner of the store. He said he never had. I asked him why not, and he said the owner would not have been interested. He said the owner had hired him to handle the issues within the store.

The former manager mentioned that the police had contacted him after the owner filed a complaint with the police department. Then he showed me a written statement he'd prepared and provided to the police. He let me read the statement, but he wouldn't let me have a copy. His statement detailed how hard he'd worked for the owner, how much he felt unappreciated, and how he was not responsible for any differences at the store.

We met for an hour and a half, discussing his roles and responsibilities as the store's manager. My impression was that, if he was the person stealing, he was pretty confident I wouldn't be able to connect the differences to him, especially since four other individuals used the same system, at times concurrently. I thought I might have an issue attributing any differences to him, at least beyond a reasonable doubt, but I thought civil remedies might be available to the owner. I knew the burden of proof in civil law was much lower than in criminal ones, so I switched strategies during our coffee-shop meeting and continued asking questions slanted toward a civil complaint. Such a lawsuit could be filed against him personally should I find that a significant loss occurred at the store. Listening to the details he provided in response to my questions, I was confident that the former manager never suspected my strategy.

When we completed the meeting, I thanked him for his time. I then met with the owner and arranged to obtain the daily bundles for the most recent two-year period. A day or two later, I received the daily bundles and secured them as evidence. We then started our analysis, comparing reports to deposits and reconciling reports from one system to the activity reported on a separate system. We charted the daily activity as well as the daily identified differences. Over the two-year period we analyzed, we identified total daily differences approximating a half million dollars.

Working with the attorney retained by the owner, we strategized how to proceed, both criminally and civilly. We agreed that the civil route was the way to start, and the attorney drafted a lawsuit against the former manager, alleging breach of fiduciary duty, statutory fraud, and other complaints. Once he'd drafted the lawsuit, the attorney summoned a state marshal to serve the lawsuit upon the former manager. The state marshal told the attorney that when she'd handed the lawsuit to the former manager, he'd been shocked. The color ran from his face, and he looked sick. The state marshal also told the attorney that she'd seen what appeared to be piles of computer reports at the former manager's house.

On that same day, a mere two hours later, we learned that the former manager had been involved in a minor single-vehicle collision and that the cab of his vehicle had caught fire. The fire department had tried to open the vehicle doors, but the former manager would not unlock them. The fire department then breached the vehicle and rescued the former manager, but not until he'd suffered significant burns and smoke inhalation. The fire department described the piles of business records and reports sitting in the vehicle. All were lost in the fire. The former manager was then flown to a burn unit, where he survived his injuries and spent a month recovering.

A month later, the former manager was discharged from the hospital and returned to his home to be cared for by his wife. After being home for a very short period of time, the former manager allegedly went into one of his vehicles parked in his driveway and fatally shot himself in the head. ▪

Unfortunately for the former manager's family, the case did not end there. Not only did they have to deal with his suicide, they also had to defend fraud claims against his estate and his wife. The former manager had left an estate with assets, and the lawsuit was revised to go after the former manager's estate to recover the funds diverted from the store. Furthermore, our investigation identified that the former manager's wife was likely a co-conspirator in the scheme and had benefited from the fraudulent activity. Thus, she was added as a defendant in the matter.

It is hard not to think about the impact and emotions the parties may feel due to the loss of the individual. As sad as it may be working on a matter after someone has killed themselves, the case must still be resolved. The fraud examiner may work with counsel to identify a new strategy to resolve the matter based on new parties added or by going in a new direction. In this case the owner wanted to recover as much of the diverted funds as possible, and because the suspect had an estate with assets, the owner wanted to collect restitution from the estate's assets. Subsequent meetings where the suspect's family was present were a bit strained, as expected, but the case was ultimately resolved for our client.

In another matter, our client was the sole owner of a local business. The owner met someone from the area who was looking for a career opportunity. The individual was young, had family roots in the community, and had served in the military. Throughout the year, the owner groomed his new employee with the goal of making him manager and ultimately part owner of the business. Toward the end of that year, we met with the owner and his attorneys to develop the owner's estate planning as well as to start succession planning. We met with the new manager on several occasions to explain what was happening and how he was benefiting from the owner's planning. The manager's wife started to work in the business as well, and the owner was happy to see his plans coming together. As the end of the year approached, we worked with the owner to determine the profitability of the business and to perform some tax planning.

It was around the same time that the business's bookkeeper received a call from a credit card company asking to speak with the business owner. The credit card company wanted to verify the owner's authorizations on recent cash advances made on the company credit card. The owner called us, saying he was not aware his business had a credit card. We also were not aware of any credit card issued or used by the business. We quickly determined that the new manager had been the individual making the cash advances. Needless to say, the owner was devastated.

The situation worsened when the bookkeeper stated that monthly rents had not been paid by the manager and his wife, who were living in one of the owner's houses. Monthly rents had also not been collected from the other tenants in the owner's other properties, which the manager had been responsible for collecting and depositing. The owner asked us to meet with the manager to discuss these new developments and obtain his story. We met with the manager, who sat silent and emotionless while we explained what we had learned. He provided no details or explanations for his actions. We then brought the manager and the owner together to continue the discussion. The owner was furious, yelling one minute and crying the next. All the manager said to the owner was, "I am sorry." Then he walked out of the building. Needless to say, he was terminated, as was his wife. We later learned that she too had been stealing almost daily from the retail store she ran for the owner.

Less than a few weeks later, the owner called us. He told us that the manager had committed suicide, leaving behind his young wife and a child. I can recall many times during the next few weeks where the memory of the young manager, whom I had interacted with many times during the year, popped into my head. When that happened, I had to stop what I was doing. It still makes me sad to think that, with everything the manager had going for him – a bright future with a new business opportunity and the comfort of a decent living – he'd resorted to stealing from the owner and then ultimately ended his own life.

Any instance of suicide within a fraud examination will affect you in some way. Depending on how many interactions you've had with the individual, the effect may be minimal or more substantive. Either way, you will think about it from time to time. Hopefully, if you are like me, you will learn from these experiences. You will become better at recognizing the signs that someone you're interacting with is considering suicide, and you will make it a point to address it.

One thing you can do is to talk to the individual about suicide, and tell them that it is not the solution. Tell them that everything can be worked out, and that nothing is worth taking one's life. Identify people the individual knows who you can share your concerns with, regardless of the reactions you may receive. Not everyone will take it seriously, until something tragic happens.

HOMICIDE

A quick discussion about homicides and fraud examinations. Sometimes homicides involve a financial motive. Other cases may involve the handling of finances of the victim after their death. A term used in the field is "red-collar" crime, referring to fraud cases that involve violence, and both suicide and homicide fit that description. Understandably, the fraud examiner should expect emotions in these cases, especially when dealing with the victim's family and friends.

In one homicide case we were involved in, a detective described the crime as an emotional assault on the victim. He told us that passion and emotions fuel many homicides.

W̲e received a call from a detective at a local police department about a matter involving a woman who had stabbed her husband multiple times. The detective told us his department needed help understanding some financial transactions and activity related to the victim, as well as the suspect and her son. The detective told us that after the woman had been arrested, her son had bailed her out using a suitcase of cash. The amount used for bail was a couple hundred thousand dollars and the police department wanted to try and figure out where the cash had originated. ▪

This case made me realize that fraud matters could result from violence, and also could be the cause for violence. Fraud examiners working outside of law enforcement agencies need to keep these truths in mind to ensure their own safety. People who are under significant stress and are highly emotional may act unpredictably, without warning, which could impact the fraud examiner's personal safety.

In one case I remember reading about in the media, the fraud examiners themselves became the victims of violent crime. In this case, two insurance fraud examiners who'd gone to an individual's house to gather information about a case were gunned down and killed by the individual.

Please consider your own safety, and that of the others working with you, while conducting any fraud examinations.

In the last chapter of this section, I discuss the stages of grieving and how they apply to fraud engagements, and introduce the concept of magical thinking.

CHAPTER EIGHT

Stages of Grief and Magical Thinking

N THE FEW YEARS I spent researching emotions and feelings in order to write this book, I found two concepts worth sharing with fraud examiners, as I believe both are applicable to fraud examinations: the stages of grieving and magical thinking. Looking back at my cases, these may have occurred in my cases.

 ## STAGES OF GRIEF

In Dr. Elisabeth Kübler-Ross's book *On Death and Dying: What the Dying Have to Teach Doctors, Nurses, Clergy & Their Own Families,*[1] she identifies five emotional stages that terminally ill patients experience:[2]

1. Denial
2. Anger
3. Bargaining
4. Depression
5. Acceptance

As I dove deeper into information on the stages of grieving, I also found what is referred to as the "Modified Kübler-Ross Model," where two additional stages have been added to the original list:[3]

1. Shock
2. Denial
3. Anger
4. Bargaining
5. Depression
6. Testing
7. Acceptance

I have to admit I didn't immediately make a connection between the stages of grieving and fraud examinations when I first came across Kübler-Ross's work. I had heard of the stages of grieving through my work volunteering on the ambulance, but only in the context of someone dying. However, as I reflected on the different engagements I'd completed, the individuals involved, and their emotional states, I started to see a correlation between the two fields. I remembered individuals I'd encountered, victims and suspects alike, who passed through similar stages during the pendency of their matter.

I first looked at the stages of grieving from the perspective of the fraud victim. Upon first learning that they have likely been the target of a financial crime, victims are often in denial about what has happened. In reaction, they try to find a more acceptable explanation for what they have just discovered. Their denial is especially understandable when they learn that the fraud perpetrator was a family member, close personal friend, or trusted advisor. I have witnessed many clients who, upon learning about a fraud, told us we were wrong, that there had to be some other explanation for their money going missing. Many denied that they had been victims and rejected the reality that a fraud had occurred.

It's easy to see why denial is the first stage in the process. Try putting yourself in the shoes of a fraud victim. You have lived modestly and saved for your retirement your entire life, working with a trusted advisor who met with you and your family at regular intervals. You received periodic reports from your advisor and the investment firms where your funds were being held in various accounts. Your trusted advisor had become like family to you, calling you on your birthday and holidays, sending cards and small gifts, and supporting your investment and planning decisions over the years. (This is the type of relationship I have with my own financial planner.)

Suppose that one day you call your advisor's office and find that the number is no longer in service. You try calling again, thinking you've misdialed, but receive the same response – the number is no longer in service. You then call your advisor's cell phone, only to be directed to their voicemail, which reports that the mailbox is full and cannot accept any further messages. You then send your advisor an email, only to have your email bounce back as undeliverable. Worry sets in, followed by panic.

You call the investment firms where your accounts were held, only to learn that your accounts were closed out two months ago, right after the quarterly reports were generated. Your investments have been sold, and the funds paid out.

Your first response will probably be to hope that this isn't what it appears to be. Your financial advisor couldn't have possibly disappeared with all of your money. Part of your brain will be searching for other possibilities. Perhaps you forgot that you had made investment changes and moved your funds to a new financial institution? Is it possible the advisor moved his office and changed his phone numbers, but you forgot?

If this happened to me, I know I would find it impossible to think that my advisor of nearly 30 years had violated my trust and stolen my money. Initially, I would be in shock and denial. Given my background and experience, I would also feel incompetent and humiliated.

Then I would progress to anger. I would think back to all the trips my advisor had taken over the years, all the golfing he'd enjoyed around the world. I would think about how my traveling paled in comparison to his, and then I would start to think about whether it was possible he had enjoyed such a wonderful life by using my funds and the funds of other clients. I would not only feel violated, I would be incredibly angry. I would want the advisor put in jail for the rest of his life. Feeling completely used, I would then want vengeance. There is no doubt that, once I knew he was the cause of my funds being missing, I would be furious.

As illustrated here, a fraud victim typically moves from denial to anger. As more details about the case become known, the individual will likely become upset at learning the details of how they were victimized. This period can be a dangerous time in any case, as individuals may act without thinking while they are angry. These impulsive actions may negatively impact their fraud investigation. An experienced fraud examiner should be careful to remind the victim in this stage not to react without first discussing their plans with the fraud examiner and their attorney.

Although a victim's anger toward the perpetrator may never subside, at some point the victim starts looking for ways to recover their funds. And although the relationship with the suspect is now over, the victim shifts gears to getting some of their money back. However, in most fraud cases, the stolen funds are gone and the chances of any decent recovery are slim to none. At this stage, the client will likely shift into the bargaining stage. If the victim can get some of their funds back, then at least they won't have suffered a total loss. The victim will still be angry, but they now see that recovering some of their money back will be better than getting nothing.

The next stages the victim will move through are depression and then acceptance.

In most fraud investigations, we look not only at the specific fraud activity that occurred, but also at other aspects of the case that result from the fraudulent activity. Often, the victim may suffer further consequences as a result of the fraudulent activity.

For example, consider a scenario where an individual within the billing department of a physician's office has been stealing insurance payments. Upon further investigation, the fraud examiner might learn that the individual also billed out for procedures that were never performed and created fictitious charges that patients paid as part of their visits. Based on these additional fraud schemes, the practice may face not only financial loss due to the theft, but additional consequences arising from the perpetrator's other actions. For example, the practice may have to refund payments to patients who paid fictitious charges. The practice may need to notify the affected insurance companies that they have provided payments for procedures that were never performed. The practice then may need to refund those payments. If federal programs such as Medicare were involved, the practice will have to notify federal agencies about the fraudulent activity, and these agencies might initiate additional investigations or audits that could result in penalties for the practice.

In the case of a financial advisor who absconds with a victim's funds, the victim's additional consequences may comes in the form of taxes. The victim may receive 1099 forms for the withdrawals made by the advisor, subjecting the victim to significant income taxes and penalties on funds that they never received or approved being removed from their accounts. Resolving these issues with the IRS can be time-consuming and exhausting.

In both these theoretical cases, each victim may look for alternative ways to resolve their matter with the least risk and exposure, only to learn that referring the activity is a compliance requirement – it's not optional. Thinking about all the possible outcomes and consequences of the fraud, the victim may move into depression.

As time goes on – and financial cases often take a long time to resolve – the victim may move into acceptance: "It is what it is." During this stage, the victim realizes there is little they can do about their situation. At this point, whatever happens with their matter is beyond their control, and all they can do is wait and deal with new developments as they occur.

If fraud matters are resolved quickly, it's easier for the victim to move toward closure and get on with their life. They may never recover their funds or fully recover emotionally, but they will at least gain closure on the matter. That is an ideal scenario, and in some cases that is exactly what happens. However, in general, the process works very slowly. Days become weeks, weeks become months, and in some cases, months become years. Fraud cases can drag on for a long time with no glimmer of closure in sight. Victims grow tired of dealing with their matter and tired of writing checks for the professionals trying to resolve their matter. The more time that passes, the more likely it is that the victim will move into depression, believing their matter will never end. In my personal experience, the longest matter to drag on lasted more than 10 years (however, in that case, there were multiple issues in multiple contexts that needed to be resolved).

The stages of grief are applicable to not only the fraud victim, but also the fraud suspect. When you first meet with a suspect and explain their situation, they are often in denial. Even when confronted with detailed facts that show they were responsible for the fraudulent activity, they typically won't accept what you tell them. As they learn more particulars about the evidence you have against them, they will continue to deny or minimize their involvement, or they'll try to implicate others for the fraud. In some cases, I have shown the suspect detailed transactions, actual check images, detailed payroll reports, and camera images of them perpetrating the activity, and they still remain in denial! Many who ultimately admit to their involvement acknowledge they are responsible but minimize the amounts we have identified. They tell us we're wrong and that there's no way the amounts are that high – and that's after we've showed them each and every transaction. They simply cannot wrap their minds around the fact that they have stolen so much money. Many suspects tell us the amount they believe they have stolen; this amount is always a fraction of what they actually diverted.

Suspects commonly move from denial to anger and rage, especially when they realize the amount of evidence against them. Many of my cases have resulted in the suspect getting angry with us or the victim. Sometimes they even blame the victim for their behavior. One suspect told us during his interview that his whole scheme was the business owner's fault. The suspect told us that he never wanted to travel out of the country, but that the owner insisted that he do so. The suspect told us his mindset changed during his trips. That's when his schemes had started, and the schemes continued for the next several years after his return. The suspect acknowledged that he had stolen a significant amount of money, but in his mind this was not his fault. He then berated the owner and identified things he believed the owner had done within the business and with employees, as if these things justified his theft. We ended up showing the suspect that he had embezzled over $1.4 million through his scheme.

In the end he ultimately took responsibility for his actions and went to prison. He is also one of a few perpetrators I've encountered in my 30 years of experience who ever apologized to the victim.

Bargaining is the next stage. It is very common for suspects to try to negotiate, avoid, or at least minimize the consequences they face and to downplay the significance of their actions. In my experience, many cases have been resolved at this juncture, when both the suspect and the victim are in the bargaining stage. At this time, the suspect takes responsibility for their actions and the victim is open to working out a settlement. The success of the endeavor at this stage will dependent greatly on the suspect's ability to make a meaningful level of restitution to the victim.

Once the suspect accepts the seriousness of what they've done, along with the potential consequences, they can easily move into depression. In the previous chapter we discussed how depression may lead to suicide. However, depression can also lead to isolation, decreased nutrition, poor hygiene, declined health, alcoholism, and substance abuse.

However, just as with victims, once a suspect realizes the inescapable consequences of the fraud they often move into acceptance. I have encountered several individuals who, once they realized the seriousness of their actions and knew they would be held accountable, simply came to accept their fate. Several suspects got divorced, became alienated from their children, and went off to prison.

So how can a fraud examiner apply the stages of grief to a fraud engagement? When the examiner is first brought onto the case, it's helpful to identify what stage of grief the individuals involved in the case are currently in. Based on my experience, the fraud examiner will not always be involved in an investigation from its inception. Although that would be ideal, the reality is that the fraud examiner can be brought in at any time during the fraud engagement. The fraud examiner's job, then, is to determine the current stage of the case and assess what has already transpired versus what remains to be done. As part of this assessment, the fraud examiner can determine the stage of grief the various individuals in the case are currently in and can then anticipate and prepare for the challenges associated with these stages.

Note: It's important to remember that the stages of grief may not always be applicable to every matter, may not occur in the expected order, and that an individual can return to a previous stage at any time. Although the stages of grief are a useful guide, they do not form a perfect template predicting what you will encounter. They are simply a guide.

The following case illustrates how a client's emotions can change based on events that occur as the fraud examination progresses.

We received a call from an attorney asking us to assist him with a matter involving a local medical practice. The attorney told us that the practice manager, who was the spouse of the primary physician in the group, had identified suspicious activity involving one of the billing staff. The attorney told us that the practice manager was unsure what the suspicious activity meant and wanted someone to come in and review it.

Prior to our initial meeting at the practice, the billing staff member had been placed on immediate administrative leave for an issue unrelated to the suspicious billing activity. When we first arrived, we met the practice manager as well as the primary physician of the group. We then asked for access to their system and records, and we secured a HIPAA agreement to ensure compliance.

We were then introduced to another member of the billing staff who shared an office with the person who had been placed on leave. We met with this woman for quite a while to gain an understanding of the practice along with its policies and financial procedures. At some point during our meeting, the woman said that she knew about the suspicious activity, so she wanted us to know that she had nothing to do with it. We asked her to explain what she knew about the activity, and she said the practice manager had asked her about it. She'd told the practice manager that she didn't know anything about it and that the practice manager should talk to the other billing person. We looked over at the empty desk and work area where her coworker typically sat.

We asked her what she knew about her coworker. She told us that when the checks were received in the mail, they were brought directly to her coworker for recording and for depositing at the bank. If there were questions about the checks being recorded or deposited, then the coworker could best answer those questions. We asked her if she thought her coworker was stealing checks rather than depositing them. She said that

that was what it looked like to her. She'd had a feeling something fishy had been happening, and so she'd started looking into the deposits long before the practice manager came to her with suspicions. She remembered on a few occasions that she had received the mail and put checks into the safe because her coworker was not in that day or had left early. She kept track of the checks and subsequently looked to see if they had been processed, posted to the patient accounts, and deposited. She had been waiting until she had enough information to bring her concerns to the practice manager. We told her she had certainly had enough information at this point to bring to the practice manager.

We then met with the practice manager and shared the information we'd just learned. To say the manager was blown away is an understatement. She said she'd always had personality differences with this staff member, mainly because the staff member acted as if she was superior to her. However, she never suspected this employee of stealing from the practice. The practice manager went out and brought in her husband, the physician, into the room. We shared our information with him as well. He was shocked and told us there had to be some other explanation. He didn't have any suspicions that anyone was stealing from the practice. He asked us to trace the deposit transactions to make sure that what we suspected was accurate.

After we combined the information the suspect's coworker had tracked with our own sampled transactions, it became clear that someone had been receiving payment checks, posting payments to patient accounts, and then diverting the checks to accounts other than the practice's bank account. Knowing it was unlikely that the suspect's coworker would report on herself, we asked her to help us locate all the records and supporting documents the suspect had maintained pertaining to payments received and deposits.

We then returned to the conference room, where we met with the physician and the practice manager. Together, we called their attorney to provide an update. As the attorney discussed potential strategies to determine the full extent of the fraud, we observed both the physician and the practice manager quickly becoming angry. Both were realizing that every dollar stolen had a personal impact on their family. Since the practice had no debt, every extra dollar collected should have gone to the physician and the practice manager. They stated that they wanted the employee prosecuted, arrested, and sent to jail. She would also be immediately terminated from the practice.

We worked with the practice manager for days and weeks, combing through deposits, trying to identify checks that had been received and then diverted. When we had sufficient evidence that a crime had been committed, we scheduled a meeting with the police to initiate a criminal investigation. We then watched as the couple's anger turned into tears, as they talked about the financial benefit the diverted funds could have had to their family. After they expressed this sadness, they then became angry again.

After a period of time, the employee was arrested for larceny, and both a civil complaint (lawsuit) and an insurance claim for employee theft were initiated. The practice recruited a new billing person, and activities in the practice resumed as usual. Days became weeks, and weeks became months, and still nothing much happened on any of the case's fronts. No trials were scheduled, and the insurance claim stalled. The practice manager called us regularly for updates, but all we had to report was that nothing new had happened. Eventually, the practice manager accepted the fact that financial cases like this drag on for what seems like forever. That was just the way it was. Over time, the practice manager's zeal to reach a resolution decreased, and her calls became fewer and fewer.

The case was ultimately resolved, but there were no winners and no fanfare. The suspect received no jail time but was ordered to make restitution. The practice manager and physician received little to no restitution, and the insurance paid on the claim, less the policy's deductible.

On a slightly separate note relating to the relationships you create and the emotions that you can encounter even after a case has ended, I share what happened next in this case.

The saddest part of this case wasn't the rollercoaster of emotions we encountered with the physician, the practice manager, and the suspect. The saddest part was that the physician went for radiological studies due to some back pain he was having, only to learn that he had multiple inoperable tumors along his spine and a limited amount of time remaining to live. He eventually had to stop working due to his illness, and he died not long afterward. He didn't live long enough to see justice for the crime against his practice, and his family was devastated by his unexpected death. We continued interacting with the practice manager for some time, showing our support, until our connection to her past became too much for her. At that point, we broke off any further communications. That case still makes me sad whenever I think about it.

If you're interested in learning more about how the stages of grief relate to fraud investigations and crime victims, I recommend exploring the following resources: "Customers Aren't the Only Victims: 5 Stages of Data Breach Grief" by Ricky Link,[4] "Coping With Victimization,"[5] and "The Emotional Stages of Divorce" by Pauline H. Tesler and Peggy Thompson.[6]

 ## MAGICAL THINKING

I first came across the term "magical thinking" in an article relating to gambling. It was a profile piece on Joanie Masot, Problem Gambling Coordinator at Advocacy Unlimited, that appeared in *Hartford Magazine* in March 2016. I had read many articles about gamblers, and I knew that gambling was often a reason someone turned to theft or fraud. However, the section of the article that caught my attention read as follows: "She gave up gambling for two years because she had no money. It gave her a false sense of control. Right out of high school in Vernon, Masot found work in human resources at a local bank. When her marriage failed, she was working for a municipality and had access to payroll insurance account for retirees. Magical thinking kicked in. [She] started embezzling."[7]

Since I hadn't heard of magical thinking before, I was intrigued to learn more about it. I was also very interested in knowing how magical thinking could lead to embezzlement or rationalize embezzlement. The article about Masot described how she had lost everything to gambling and turned to embezzling the town's retiree insurance funds to feed her addiction. However, the article failed to sufficiently define magical thinking. I decided I had to do more reading on the topic, since I had seen embezzlement cases where gambling was the reason the suspect cited for turning to stealing.

One publication I found was called "The Year of Magical Thinking: Fraud, Loss, and Grief," by Jayne W. Barnard,[8] which was based in part on the book *The Year of Magical Thinking* by Joan Didion. The publication not only provided a definition for magical thinking, it also compared grieving a financial loss to grieving the loss of a family member. It also offered a less traditional view on the stages of grieving, giving the reader more than one perspective to consider.

According to the *Encyclopedia Britannica*, "magical thinking" is "the belief that one's ideas, thoughts, actions, words, or use of symbols can influence the course of events in the material world. Magical thinking presumes a causal link between one's inner, personal experience and the external physical world.[9] In an article called "Ta-Da! Magical Thinking Explained," author Crystal Raypole defines magical thinking as "the idea that you can influence the outcome of specific events by doing something that has no bearing on the circumstances."[10] Raypole provides examples, such as wearing a lucky piece of clothing to ensure things go your way. She compares these practices to superstitions. I figure since I still follow some of those superstitions today (such as the idea that a black cat crossing my path will bring bad luck), I also fall into the category of magical thinkers.

According to a five-part series entitled "Unresolved Gambling Treatment Options,"[11] magical thinking is defined as "a mistaken belief that one thing has an influence on something else, when actually the two are not connected."[12] This publication cites many examples of gamblers who use magical thinking. For example, an individual might play a slot machine for an hour, cash in his winnings, and then return to the same slot machine, using different money this time to try and fool the slot machine into thinking that the gambler was a different person.

Thinking back through my years, I could not remember any case where the suspect told me that the reason they stole or committed fraud was because something or someone made them do it. Nor could I remember a case where a fraudster associated their behavior with some other event or object, like they only stole during full moons or on odd days of the month that fell on Mondays and Fridays. In my mind and based on my experiences, I failed to connect Magical Thinking with fraud.

RATIONALIZATION

As I read about magical thinking, though, I saw parallels between it and rationalization. Rationalization is a key element in the fraud triangle developed through the works of Donald R. Cressey in his book *Other People's Money*.[13] Most of us working in the fraud field simply refer to the three corners of the triangle as opportunity, pressure, and rationalization.

Cressey's hypothesis is that: "Trusted persons become trust violators when they conceive of themselves as having a financial problem which is non-shareable, are aware this problem can be secretly resolved by violation of the position of financial trust, and are able to apply to their own conduct in that situation verbalizations which enable them to adjust their conceptions of themselves as trusted persons with their conceptions of themselves as users of the entrusted funds or property."[14]

The *Merriam-Webster Dictionary* defines rationalization as "a way of describing, interpreting, or explaining something (such as bad behavior) that makes it seem proper, more attractive, etc."[15] Synonyms include *reasoning, justification,* and *explanation.* My interpretation is that rationalization is an individual's ability to make something they did or are about to do seem proper and acceptable, when in fact it is wrong, illegal, or immoral. The individual needs to convince themselves that they are not a bad person and are not doing anything wrong, which helps them internalize the idea that their behavior and actions are proper.

I recalled many cases where the suspect rationalized their behavior during meetings to discuss the details of their case. Borrowing funds, taking advances, paying themselves what they believed they were entitled, and using funds because the owners did it were all common rationalizations. Many fraudsters complained about the long hours they worked and how they were unappreciated and underpaid for their efforts. Entitlement comes to mind in most cases.

Based on my experience and limited research, I concluded that rationalization is different from magical thinking, but I still had to contend with the very first article I read, written by the gambler who used the term magical thinking as she described turning to embezzlement to fuel her gambling addiction.

In conducting this research, I was brought back to my college classes on psychology, sociology, and criminology – courses I had completed over 30 years ago. I had to remind myself that I was a fraud examiner and forensic accountant, not a psychologist. I concluded that magical thinking was not necessarily the most appropriate term to describe why Joanie Masot's gambling addiction caused her to turn to embezzling the retiree's insurance funds. Perhaps what was meant was that Ms. Masot's gambling was driven by magical thinking, and that she turned to embezzling to fuel her addiction.

My job in writing this book is to relate magical thinking to the emotions a fraud examiner could encounter on a fraud engagement. I will let you, the reader, determine if there is any correlation between rationalization, a component of the fraud triangle and a key element in most fraud cases, and magical thinking. My conclusion is that magical thinking and rationalization do not really have much to do with each other. However, I chose to include information on both in this chapter because I think they both add to a fraud examiner's understanding of client emotions and provide insight into the fraudster's thought process while conducting their activity.

Hopefully, by this point in the book, you will recognize that client emotions are a part of every fraud engagement. As we move into the last section of the book, I depart from discussing the types of emotions that you may encounter and dive into identifying strategies you can use to address client emotions and actions.

END NOTES

1. Elisabeth Kübler-Ross, *On Death and Dying: What the Dying Have to Teach Doctors, Nurses, Clergy, and Their Own Families* (Scribner: New York, 1969).
2. Ibid.
3. Zawn Villines, "Shock and Testing: Two More Twists on the Road to Grief Recovery?" *Good-Therapy* (blog), March 14, 2019, https://www.goodtherapy.org/blog/shock-testing-two-more-twists-on-road-to-grief-recovery-0314197.
4. Ricky Link, "Customers Aren't the Only Victims: 5 Stages of Data Breach Grief," *DarkReading*, February 25, 2015, https://www.darkreading.com/operations/customers-arent-the-only-victims-5-stages-of-data-breach-grief/a/d-id/1319216.
5. "Coping With Victimization," Essex County Prosecutor's Office, Office of Victim-Witness Advocacy, accessed January 11, 2021, http://www.njecpo.org/vw/sevenstages.php.
6. Pauline Tesler and Peggy Thompson, "The Emotional Stages of Divorce," WomansDivorce .com, accessed January 11, 2021, https://www.womansdivorce.com/emotional-stages-of-divorce.html.
7. Donna Larcen, "After Gambling Addiction and Prison, Joanie Masot Now Helps Other Problem Gamblers Recover," *Hartford Magazine*, March 2016, https://www.courant.com/hartford-magazine/hc-hm-joan-masot-20160229-story.html.
8. Jayne W. Barnard, "The Year of Magical Thinking: Fraud, Loss, and Grief," *Law and Psychology Review*, 2014: 1–44, https://scholarship.law.wm.edu/facpubs/1719.
9. Brian Vandenberg, "Magical Thinking," *Encyclopedia Brittanica*, accessed January 11, 2021, https://www.britannica.com/science/magical-thinking.
10. Crystal Raypole, "Ta-Da! Magical Thinking Explained," *Healthline*, February 25, 2020, https://www.healthline.com/health/magical-thinking.
11. APTPG, "Unresolved Gambling Treatment Issues, Part V: The Magical Thinking of the Compulsive Gambler," The Association of Professionals Treating Problem Gambling (APTPG), accessed January 11, 2021, https://www.aptpg.org/resources-information.
12. Ibid.
13. Donald R. Cressey, *Other People's Money* (Montclair, NJ: Patterson Smith, 1973).
14. Ibid.
15. "Rationalization," *Merriam-Webster Dictionary*, accessed January 11, 2021, https://www .merriam-webster.com/dictionary/rationalization.

PART THREE

Client Emotions: Strategies Toward Success

CHAPTER NINE

Preparing for Client Emotions

THIS CHAPTER FOCUSES ON you, the fraud examiner, since you will be at the forefront of dealing with client emotions. You will be the one clients call, email, and text. As a part of your involvement in the case, you have showed them you are interested. You listened and empathized with them as they explained their situation, so you are naturally going to set yourself apart from others involved in their matter. Thus, you will be the one they turn to with questions, stresses, and crises. You'll also be the one they contact when they are feeling down, anxious, agitated, frustrated, depressed, and just about every other emotion you can imagine.

You are the one clients will expect to immediately respond to voice messages, emails, and texts. Clients often perceive themselves to be the most important part of your world. In their minds, they are your only client. They will call your office and ask to speak with you, and if you're not at your desk, they'll ask your coworkers to find you. If you're in a meeting, they'll ask your staff to interrupt you or slip you a note to let you know they're waiting on the phone. They may claim their matter is time-sensitive or an emergency. They can drive your staff insane unless you've established clear guidelines for your staff to follow.

These calls, voice messages, emails, and texts often arrive at inopportune times. Clients don't just stress out during normal business hours – they stress at nights, on holidays, and over weekends. Thus, when they want to connect with you, they'll send messages in the middle of the night or the earliest hours of the day. If they are awake and want to discuss the issues that are worrying them, they won't hesitate to reach out. These types of communication force you to decide whether to respond immediately or wait until later.

It's frustrating to realize, as you listen to or read these messages, that clients are inquiring about issues you've previously explained, sometimes on the same day or even a half dozen other times during their case. You'll ask yourself why the client is writing about the same issues over and over. The answer, simply, is this: Many individuals feel compelled to rehash the same issues right through to the resolution of their matter – and, in some cases, even after their case is resolved. Needless to say, this style of communication can become maddening.

The following fraud case illustrates how frequent and taxing client communication can be.

We were working with a woman who had divorced her husband. She alleged he had committed fraud during their divorce by underreporting his assets and earnings. The woman's attorney had engaged us to analyze the ex-husband's business and determine how much money he made through the business. Their divorce called for him to pay his ex-wife a small amount each month, and our client was certain, based on her husband's lifestyle, that he earned much more than he had reported to the court. Our client complained that she could barely pay her bills. Meanwhile, her ex-husband was out purchasing new boats and go-carts and living a pretty good life. He had since remarried someone younger whom he'd met through his business. The court had awarded the couple joint custody of their daughter, who was a minor. The woman explained that the divorce had been very bitter, that her ex-husband was a liar and a cheat, and that they both still hated each other.

When we went to the ex-husband's business to review his financial records, he was not happy to have us there. He was rather unpleasant to us and, even after I had explained my procedures, referred to me as "disingenuous." As we scanned his bank and credit-card statements, we saw that personal purchases had been made through the business. We also saw that there were gaps in sequentially numbered sales transactions in his reports. We asked him about both issues and told him that the identified items would increase his available funds to pay alimony and child support. Displeased with our findings, he tried to have his attorney convince the judge that our findings should be precluded from the matter.

However, he was unsuccessful, so negotiations commenced between his attorney and his wife's attorney. In the meantime, our client was elated that we'd been able to show that his income was so much greater than he'd reported.

After a period of back-and-forth negotiating, both parties needed to make a decision about the case. They could either agree to the new compensation amount, which would result in higher alimony and child support payments from the ex-husband, or take the matter to trial, where it would be subject to the judge's final decision. The ex-husband risked tax exposure if he were audited, since he had deducted the personal expenses paid through his business on his business's tax returns.

Finally, the ex-husband's attorney made an offer in an attempt to settle the matter. The woman's alimony would increase fourfold, and the child support would continue until the couple's daughter turned 18. The woman called me to discuss the offer. She was reluctant to accept it because she knew her ex-husband would never pay the full amount. In addition, she said that if he was willing to pay the higher amount, it was likely he had even more income that he hadn't disclosed. Perhaps he was taking his store's sales and depositing them into a bank account we didn't know about. She wanted to take her ex-husband to trial and put him in jail for all the time he'd underpaid her after their divorce.

I tried to explain to her that if she went the trial route and succeeded in putting her ex-husband in jail, his business would end, as would his cash flows, and he wouldn't be able to pay *any* alimony or child support. If that happened, she would be worse off than when she had been receiving the reduced amount of alimony.

However, the woman was angry with her ex-husband as well as with the divorce court, which had relied on his lower reported income when initially awarding her alimony. She felt her ex-husband had pulled off his fraud without any consequences. She said she was not going to accept his offer and settle the matter.

We then received a call from her attorney, who asked us why his client wouldn't take the deal. If she accepted it, her alimony would be four times what she'd previously received, and it was a great return on her investment in the post-divorce investigation. I told him she wouldn't accept on principle, because she felt her ex-husband had suffered no consequences for the long period of time when she'd barely gotten by on a small amount of alimony. The attorney was frustrated.

Hours after those calls took place, I received a long email from the woman, who told me the story of her breakup with her ex-husband, from the time she'd learned of his affair all the way through the divorce to the present time. I had heard this account several times at meetings and on calls, but now I was hearing it again. When I finished reading her email, I sent her a short response: "Please think about the changes you could make in your life when you receive four times as much each month, and I will call you in the morning."

Later that night, I checked my email and saw I'd received a brief email from the woman, indicating that she had left me a voicemail. As much as I wanted to ignore it until tomorrow, I listened to her message. In the voicemail, she reiterated how terrible things had been for her and her daughter since the divorce, while her ex-husband had been living a very extravagant lifestyle. She said that if she took the settlement without holding him accountable, it wouldn't be fair. It was a rather lengthy message. Ultimately, I decided not to respond. I would address her message in the morning.

The next morning, I sent the woman an email letting her know I was in the office if she wanted to call me. Later that morning, she called, and I asked her how her day was going. She didn't seem too happy, but she wasn't yelling either. I asked her if she had thought more about the offer. She said she had spoken to one of her girlfriends, and the girlfriend had told her to hold out for more money. She mentioned that her girlfriend had received more money in her divorce, so her girlfriend felt she was entitled to more than what the ex-husband was presently offering.

I told her that, unless she knew the specific circumstances of her girlfriend's divorce, the chances were slim that her girlfriend's situation was exactly like her own. Judges make decisions following general guidelines but adjust their final decisions based on the facts and issues specific to each case. I told her it could be dangerous to listen to the advice of friends over the advice of her attorney.

My client asked me what I thought she should do. I told her that, based on the financial information we'd analyzed, increasing her income fourfold would have a significant impact on her lifestyle and would also clear up the debt she'd accumulated since her divorce. I advised her to think carefully about what the increased amount could do for her and her daughter, and to separate those possibilities from getting even with her ex-husband. I told her that, in large part, she had already won. She had shown the attorneys that her ex-husband was a liar and a cheat.

The woman said she needed time to think about the offer.

Over the next few days, we spoke or emailed about the same issues at least two dozen times. Each time, the woman asked the same questions, and each time I provided the same responses. Just when I thought she was ready to settle, I would receive a new voice message or email. She flip-flopped, day after day, telling me in one message that she had accepted the offer and then rejecting it in the next. Finally, she accepted the offer and settled the case. She then called to thank me for being patient and explaining things to her over, and over, and over . . .

Over time, as I continued to learn from experience, I developed strategies for dealing with situations like these. The following strategies have served me well for nearly 30 years, and these best practices may help you better manage communications with emotional clients.

 ## DEVELOP YOUR OWN APPROACH

If you want to be responsive to clients while maintaining your sanity, you need to develop an approach that identifies, addresses, and manages client emotions. In order to develop this approach, start with an honest assessment of who you are. How much patience do you have? How much time do you want to spend talking with or responding to clients? And what other resources do you have available to deal with client emotions?

Through nearly 30 years of interacting with clients, I have grown more patient and understanding than when I first started out in this field. Now I believe my responsiveness is second to none. I deal with good news or bad as quickly as I can, getting on top of an issue before moving onto the next crisis. My approach has been to respond to client communications as quickly as practical, as to not let the client's anxiety grow. I have been very successful in talking clients down and getting them back to a more relaxed state of mind. However, my current approach is based on years of practice and experience, and I remember interactions early in my career that did not go so well, even when I deployed what I thought at the time were thoughtful measures. All you can do is learn from your experiences and try to do better the next time.

In my firm, our present resources are limited to me and one other staff member. Although we regularly employ interns, providing them with opportunities to gain experience in this field, we never let interns respond to client messages or address client emotions. In my firm, I primarily handle client emotions and responses, with my staff member also providing some coverage.

In a larger firm with more resources, a fraud examiner may have more options to minimize or delegate client interactions. In larger law firms, for example, attorneys often attend meetings and handle certain aspects of a matter but then use an administrative assistant or paralegal to handle other client interactions. This approach can work well, especially if the attorney doesn't possess the necessary patience and people skills to deal with clients. However, this approach will only be successful under the following conditions: (1) there are people available to whom the attorney can delegate these responsibilities; (2) the attorney remains accessible as needed and informed of all interactions between the client and the delegated person; (3) the client perceives that the delegated person and the attorney are working as a team; (4) the client does not feel that they have been pawned off; and (5) the delegated person possesses the skills to address client emotions. The same requirements hold true for larger investigative firms and internal fraud departments.

In my experience, some firms that have taken this approach have had success with it, while others haven't. The amount of success has largely been dependent on the attorney and those the attorney chose to delegate functions and communications. The clients who were unhappy being handled this way made sure to complain about it to us throughout the engagement (not that there was anything we could do about it).

Whatever approach you decide to take, your first step should be to set clear expectations at the outset of each engagement.

SET CLIENT EXPECTATIONS

In Chapter 2, I discussed setting client expectations. This step should be a two-part process that involves: (1) setting their expectations for you, the fraud examiner; and (2) setting their expectations about their matter. While you do want to be responsive to and understanding of your client's needs, you don't want clients to become demanding and unreasonable. When clients get angry and frustrated, they ramp up communications and matters spiral out of control until you can bring them back to a sense of reason. It can be difficult, if not impossible, to get clients to act reasonably during highly emotional times, so it is critical that at the outset of an engagement, you find logical communication solutions that work for you both.

At the onset of your involvement, you should outline expectations with the client, the attorney, and anyone else involved in the matter. Discuss not only your approach and the services you provide, but also how and when you will respond to voice messages, emails, and texts. At this point, you must decide whether you are going to provide clients with your cell phone number (a decision that I discuss in more detail shortly). If you are going to have someone else return messages or emails on your behalf, introduce that person to the client and others and explain how you work as a team to remain informed. This initial conversation may be the one opportunity you have to address these issues while the clients are calm and rational, before you start working on the assignment.

Afterwards, as you work on the engagement, if the client communicates frustration or anger because you weren't available or they didn't receive a fast-enough response, you can remind them of that first meeting and your outlined expectations. The key is for you to honor the expectations you established at that first meeting.

You should set the client's expectations at the onset of every engagement, with guidelines based on your prior experience resolving similar matters. Even when the outcome of a new case appears obvious, you must remember that all cases are subject to unpredictable results. Educate every new client about the process, and identify challenges that may arise. This discussion will help the client decide whether or how to pursue a matter. List out the pros and the cons of each possible avenue toward resolution, and review in detail the costs and benefits of spending the time, effort, and funds on this undertaking. Remember that your client is a consumer who wants to make an informed decision about this contemplated transaction.

ESTABLISH GROUND RULES

Establish ground rules at your first meeting with a new client, right at the inception of the potential engagement and before accepting the matter or performing any procedures. My firm always establishes ground rules in the very first meeting, the "meet-and-greet" session where the client decides whether they want to work with us, and vice versa. As I've said earlier, one of the luxuries of running a practice as an independent fraud examiner is that I can choose which clients I want to accept and which I want to refer to another resource. I can remember meetings where I walked away from a case, as well as ones where I ran. In other professional contexts, however, the fraud examiner may be an employee of an organization and so may have less control over the cases they take on.

At the first meeting, I discuss how I typically communicate with clients, and I give the client a realistic expectation of when they can expect to receive responses from me. I ask the client for their contact information, and I ask them to describe their communication expectations. I provide them with our firm's business hours and tell them that there is usually someone available to answer our phones during those hours. The person answering the phone knows how to reach me when I am out of the office if something comes up that is time-sensitive. I also tell clients that we can react to an unexpected situation that occurs outside of normal business hours and that we often review and respond to emails throughout most evenings and weekends.

I discuss our physical offices and tell the client that, due to the nature of our cases, we customarily do not conduct unplanned visits or meetings. Often, as we work, we spread out the materials from a case on our conference room table. When we are working on larger cases, the case files may be stacked in piles on the floor or along the walls while they are sorted and organized. An unplanned visit not only disrupts our schedule, but it also disrupts the case we are currently working on.

Addressing this topic up front has helped us reduce surprise visits by clients and decrease the necessity of dealing with in-person crises. Thankfully, when these situations have occurred, they have been limited to a few instances.

ENSURE YOUR SAFETY

We must consider safety issues when someone in an emotional state shows up unexpectedly at our office. If I am not present at the time of their visit, my staff will have to deal with the emotional client on their own. I've found it's best to tell clients up front not to show up without an appointment.

I can remember a few instances of an emotional client showing up unannounced at our office. None of the encounters went well, and most involved screaming, yelling, and crying. Partly as a result of these encounters, we've taken steps to maintain tight security at our firm. Our main office has solid entrance doors and glass sidelights. One door acts as our main entrance, and one as a private entrance at the back of our space. Both entrance doors contain biometric deadbolt locksets, which allow us to come and go without using keys, and both display a sign that simply reads, "Private." The name of our firm is not displayed on our doors, nor is it on the building directories in the lobby. We had a security assessment performed on our space, and as a direct result we treated our sidelights so that they were no longer transparent. Now, it's possible to see shadows through the sidelights, but no one can simply look into our office any longer. We've also installed door scopes – oversized peepholes – into our solid doors. These are covered on the inside when not in use, and they allow us to see an 180-degree view of the hallways outside our doors. All of these enhancements help us when there is an unexpected knock at the door.

The following event is what led to us having larger peepholes installed in our doors to allow us to see who was at our doors, and to implement other measures to ensure our safety when in our office. They were installed and implemented the very next day after this event.

I was sitting in the conference room being interviewed for an article about my firm. Suddenly and unexpectedly, there was a loud pounding on the entrance door, just feet from where we were sitting. Startled, the writer and I both jumped out of our chairs. I signaled to the writer to remain seated and quiet, then I opened the peephole to see who was there. I was shocked to see a casually dressed man of gigantic proportions, standing inches away from my door, looking right at the peephole.

Just then, I heard a loud pounding on our back door, just as hard as the pounding on the front door. I realized there had to be two people outside, each one standing at a different door. I quietly walked away from the front door and toward the back of the office, as the man at the front door started pounding again. I picked up the phone and dialed 911.

I told the dispatcher my address and said there were two large men outside my office pounding on my doors and I had no idea who they were. I described the man outside our front door and asked the dispatcher to send the police quickly. I then sat back down with the writer and waited. We heard one more round of pounding on each door, and then the hallway went silent.

It seemed like eternity before I heard movement in the hallway. Then, two or three shadows appeared at my door. I heard a knock and then the words I'd been waiting to hear: "It's the police." I quickly looked out the peephole: There were three police officers at my door. Opening the door, I glanced down the hallway to my left and saw two more police officers walking toward my office. My heart was racing. I asked the police if they'd caught the two men as they'd exited the building.

Much to my disappointment, the officers said they hadn't seen any men in the building on their way up to my office. I told them that, given the timing, they had to have passed the men who'd been pounding on my doors. One of the officers asked me what the men looked like, and I described the large man I'd seen. The policeman said they had passed the two guys as they'd entered the building, but they hadn't stopped them. The policemen then ran down the hall and toward the parking lot. A few minutes later, one police officer returned and said they hadn't located the two men. The men must have driven away before the police got back to our parking lot. "Great," I thought – I'd told the dispatcher there were two large men menacing my office, and the police had run right by them on their way here.

Now I had no idea who these men were or why they'd come to my office. I wondered if they'd be coming back again, since they must have thought I wasn't in the office just then.

After a few sleepless nights and a few days of looking around the parking lot each time I arrived or left the office, I remained in a state of heightened awareness. Finally, after reflecting on my current cases and the clients associated with them, I came up with a theory about what had happened. We had recently been retained by an attorney to help review the financial records of a restaurant to determine whether improper financial activity had occurred. We hadn't yet performed any services, but the client had accumulated a fair amount of records that their attorney asked we safeguard so that nothing happened to them. We had secured those records within our office.

We had not yet met any of the individuals involved in the case and had only accepted the engagement based on our conversation with the attorney. That day, I called the attorney and asked him to describe the individuals involved in the case. He said two of the owners of the restaurant in question were also bail bondsmen, and he described them as large, crude men. He said they were brothers who were angry with his client, another owner in their restaurant. When I heard this, I knew it had to be the two brothers who had pounded on my doors – but I wondered why they had showed up at my office, as we had yet to perform any services for our client, except for storing the records.

When the client's attorney made a call to opposing counsel, opposing counsel confirmed that it was the two brothers who had pounded on my doors, treating the encounter like one of their bail enforcement raids and covering both doors so I couldn't escape. Opposing counsel said that the brothers thought there was a meeting at my office, so they had shown up for the meeting. They'd left when they realized they had the wrong day. I told the attorney that was nonsense (although that was not the word I used). There had never been a meeting set in the matter, let alone a meeting in my office. If the brothers had been there for a meeting, they would have politely knocked on my main door. There would have been no need for them to pound on both office doors simultaneously.

I asked the attorney to call opposing counsel again and deliver a message. If we saw the brothers at my building, in my building, or out in the parking lot, I would have them arrested. I had already put the police on notice.

My best guess is that the brothers came to my office to intimidate us and gain access to their restaurant records. Both attorneys on the case knew the records were being stored in my office. I wondered what would have happened if I had not been in the office that day. What if my staff members had been there alone when the two goons showed up? When I told this story to my staff, I told them they were never to open the door to strangers, and if something like that ever happened again, they were to call the police. Period. ▪

Since that encounter, my firm has incorporated additional safety measures to ensure that if something like that ever happens again, we remain safe until the police arrive at our office. We also have cameras in the building on all floors that we can now access and monitor.

KEEP CLIENTS INFORMED

One practice I adhere to is providing regular updates to clients as each engagement progresses. Depending on the attorney's position on communications, we usually send updates via email to counsel and the client, keeping both abreast of our progress as well as any issues we've encountered. Knowing that these communications could be discoverable at a later date (meaning the other side could require them be produced), we keep the updates brief and general and do not include any preliminary findings.

Although some of our fraud engagements have lasted several days or weeks, the average case spans many months. Still others have dragged out into years, especially when litigation was involved. During cases, our brief updates act as a diary, tracking our efforts on a matter. They can also prove extremely useful when refreshing our memory about a case, especially if long periods have passed since we last worked on it. Commonly, we will start a case, identify the additional information we need, and then wait for the information to be provided for analysis. When that information is provided within a short period of time, we still have the case details fresh in our minds. However, it has not been my general experience that we receive requested records in a timely fashion. Often, there is a long delay before the records are provided, if they're provided at all.

During this waiting period, we move on to working on other cases. After a while, the details of our open cases tend to blur together. When our attention is called back to a case after a long period of time, we read our updates to get up to speed on where we left off. We save our updates and communications in a matter-specific folder on our server, organized by attorney and segregated from other matters. This strategy makes it easy for us to stay organized and informed. Our updates also help us when an attorney or a client calls and says we were supposed to do something that we didn't. We then go back through our updates and forward the client our last communication, specifying where we left off and what information we were waiting on. Our updates have cleared up much ambiguity in our clients' recollections.

BE WARY OF YOUR CELL PHONE: SET BOUNDARIES (AND EXPECT THEM TO BE CROSSED)

In each engagement, you will have to decide whether to provide your cell phone number to a client and others involved in a matter. If you are like me and you work in the field more than in the office, your cell phone is the best way for clients to get in touch with you. Cell phones are very useful when I'm often out of the office. Even if I'm in a client meeting or unavailable, I can see a text or missed call on my phone and can respond as soon as I'm available again. I find that it's very efficient for clients and attorneys to call or text me on my cell phone, as long as they don't abuse their access to me.

As with every other means of communication the fraud examiner uses, the cell phone comes along with a risk that a client will use it to become intrusive. Given the ease, accessibility, and informality of cell phones, clients can easily call or text at all hours, including nights, weekends, and holidays. Not only that, clients also expect to receive rapid responses to their messages. It seems clients use their cellular devices – more so than voice messages and emails – 24/7, and they expect everyone else to do the same. Often, they will send a short text (the bait, if you will) to see if you'll respond. If you make the mistake of responding, then their texts start pouring in. When you receive these texts and choose not to respond, they will send more texts asking why you're not responding, because they know you have your device with you! Their emotions will continue to escalate until you set firm boundaries.

My advice to you is to carefully consider the people to whom you provide your cell phone number. Do not provide your cell number to just any client, even if they ask for it. In addition, don't preprint your cell phone number on your business cards, unless your strategy is to provide it to everyone who receives your card. My cell number is not on my business card, nor is it included in my email signature. I choose to provide it only to those I want to have it.

A client may ask you directly for your cell phone number. If you choose not to provide it, you need to be prepared to tell the client why. For example, you can tell them that you only use emails for communicating with clients, to better ensure that their attorney remains updated on the communications. This is a very valid reason. Texts are much less formal than email, and unless the client's attorney wants to provide their cell phone number and be included in text conversations (which they will not), then the attorney will not see the communication. Some clients will understand this reasoning, but others will insist on having your cell phone number in case they need to reach you when you're out of the office. These clients are likely the people who will abuse the privilege of having your personal number. You will need to decide on a case-by-case basis what to tell a client if they insist on having your cell number.

Keep in mind that if you call a client's cell phone from your cell phone, your client will capture and save that number for future use, even if you've previously told them you don't use your cell phone for client matters. Once a client has your cell phone number, you'll start receiving calls and texts from them, which may come as a surprise if you didn't expect them to have access to that number.

If you choose to provide clients with your cell phone number, set clear boundaries with them at the time that you give it to them. Tell them that they cannot call your cell phone at any time of day. Tell them that your work hours are 8 a.m. to 5 p.m., Monday through Friday, and that you have a life outside of work. Tell them that they should not call or text you outside of those hours unless you've given them advance permission. In addition, tell them that if they do call or text you, they may not receive an immediate response. You have other client commitments, and you will return their call or text as soon as possible. Most cell phones offer predefined responses to let callers know you are busy, such as, "I am in a meeting and can't talk right now." I recommend using these messages to indicate to clients that you are unable to immediately respond.

Thankfully, most clients will honor your parameters and respect your personal time. However, when dealing with emotional clients, you should expect that some will charge right across your boundaries and call or text whenever they want to speak with you, regardless of the time or day. When you don't respond immediately, they will continue sending messages, even if they know you're spending the day with your family. They may even say in their message: "I know you're spending the day with your family, but ..."

You have to decide how you will respond to this intrusion into your personal time. My advice is to remind your client about the boundaries you initially established. When I encounter intrusive clients in my cases, I respond by telling them I will not be able to connect with them today. I tell them that at a later time, I'll connect with them and address their issue. Afterwards, I always follow up when I said I would.

Is this a hard-and-fast rule for all of my clients? No. Once I come to know my clients and their cases, I may choose to talk to them immediately or return a text even at nights, on weekends, or during my personal time. In those instances, I will likely limit the duration of our conversation so the client does not consume my night or weekend. However, I will get enough information from them in order to ascertain their question and then tell them we can discuss the matter further when I am in the office.

Occasionally, you may encounter a client who simply ignores your boundaries and continues texting you. They may say something like, "I know, but this will only take a minute . . ." This is a client who demonstrates no regard for your personal time and space. In their mind, their issue is just as important as anything else you have going on in your life. I tell these clients that my phone will be turned off and I will reply to them as soon as I can, but that likely will not happen until I return the office. By responding this way, I know that the client's anxiety may continue to build. When we next speak, they may be agitated, stressed, and upset. However, I have to be careful not to let their emotional state alter my life. I cannot be available to them 24/7. Emotional clients can consume your life if you let them.

When I do eventually speak with these clients, I let them vent, and then I tell them that if I didn't separate my business from my personal life, I wouldn't have a personal life. You have to set boundaries to keep your clients, your family, and yourself happy, and you have to enforce those boundaries. If you don't, you risk going out of your mind.

THE LONGEST TEXTS YOU WILL EVER RECEIVE

One last thing about client communication: When a client sends you a text that takes several seconds just to scroll through, it can be painful to read through this essay on your mobile device, searching for their question or ultimate point. Cell phone screens tend to be smaller and harder to read, and texts were intended to be short, abbreviated communications, not detailed dissertations. I find these texts very draining to read.

After scrolling through a long text, I text the client back, telling them that my device is having issues scrolling. I then ask that they copy and paste their message into an email to me. I have found that clients will comply and that it's far easier for me to read long messages on a computer than on my cell phone. I can also then delete the client's text from my phone and forward their email to their attorney.

LOOK FOR OPPORTUNITIES FOR CATHARSIS

The final section of this chapter addresses the client's need for catharsis. It's important for the fraud examiner to know and understand the client's goals in engaging a fraud examiner. Often, the client is not only looking for the facts, but also for someone to explain why the fraud happened. They also often want the perpetrator to apologize for their actions. In many cases the victim told us at the onset of our involvement that if the loss was not too significant and the reason the person committed fraud was to put food on their table, feed their kids, or provide a life for their children, that would influence how they chose to resolve the matter. Hence, they needed to know why the person committed the fraud.

My experience has been that, unlike in other types of crimes, in fraud cases the victim rarely gets an opportunity to confront the perpetrator. If the matter is prosecuted criminally, most perpetrators take a plea agreement and few go through the trial process. In some cases, an employer may have an initial meeting with a suspect when the first signs of fraud are discovered, but the goal of that meeting is often only to put the person on leave. That early in the case, the employer may not be fully aware of the extent of the fraud. Often, this meeting is frustrating for the employer because the suspect provides few or no responses to the employer's questions. Similarly, in cases where a family member commits fraud against another family member, the family members often don't talk or meet. Instead, they retain attorneys to resolve the matter.

In some cases the fraud is pursued through civil actions, and in this case individuals do have an opportunity to interact. However, less than 5 percent of cases go to trial, and many are resolved through arbitration, mediation, and settlement, often with attorneys speaking on behalf of their clients. If a trial occurs, the best a client can do is provide their attorney with questions to ask the suspect and then listen to the provided responses.

The process can leave clients with many unanswered questions and frustrations. The question that may never be answered is "Why?"

In many of my cases, the victim has at least three goals in pursuing their matter. First, they want their money back, as well as to recoup the costs of hiring attorneys and fraud examiners to put the case together. Second, they want to know why the person did what they did. Why did the perpetrator take advantage of the victim? Finally, the client wants an apology. I have found this outcome the hardest to obtain for my clients. Over the course of my career, I can count on my fingers the number of individuals who apologized to the person they'd stolen from – and I have investigated over 300 embezzlement cases and countless other fraud-related matters.

I remember nearly all of the cases where an apology was provided. The following case is one where I felt the individual's apology was genuine.

The controller of a small manufacturing business was found to have stolen over $1 million from the company. We collected records and obtained replacement bank statements in order to reconstruct what had happened. It was not an overly complex embezzlement scheme, but since the owner of the business had relied entirely on the controller for all financial aspects of his business, it went undetected for several years. Once the theft was discovered, the owner was understandably angry.

As part of determining the full extent of the loss, the owner demanded that the controller meet with him and his attorneys to answer questions about the fraud.

This meeting was very awkward, since the owner and the controller had formerly been friends. The owner started the meeting by asking the controller why he'd stolen. The controller said that one transaction had led to another, and then the scheme had simply gotten out of control. Toward the end of the meeting, the owner asked the controller if he had anything else he wanted to add to his story. The controller became very emotional and wept. He apologized for his actions and for violating the owner's trust. He said he would take full responsibility for his actions. I felt that the controller was truly sincere and that he understood the impact of his actions on the owner and the company. ▧

Sometimes, however, the perpetrator's apology is not genuine, and the person providing it merely wants to achieve a settlement in the matter. I can recall one such case where the suspect's apology turned out to be disingenuous. This case is also a great example of how emotions can change throughout a fraud investigation.

The sole owner of a small business was grooming one of his younger employees to take over his company. For two years, the owner and the younger employee did nearly everything together, both at work and outside of the business. Over time, the owner shared more details about running his company with his younger employee, and discussions were underway to transfer ownership of the company's stock to the younger employee, at no cost to him. The owner had already drafted documents to accomplish this.

At the end of their second season together, the owner learned from his bookkeeper that his employee had not paid rent on the house he'd been living in for nearly a year. The employee had told the bookkeeper that the house's owner knew about the lack of payment and had said that it was alright, but in fact that discussion never occurred. The business owner then remembered that earlier in the year he had loaned his employee thousands of dollars to help the employee with medical costs – or so he had been told.

The business owner was working with his bookkeeper to understand why the company's profit was close to $100,000 below its profit in previous years when there had been no changes in customers or volume. The bookkeeper then received an unsolicited call from the business's credit-card company, alerting her that someone had been making daily cash advances on the company credit card. She shut the card off and updated the owner.

The owner asked me to meet with his employee to discuss these issues, so we all had lunch together. The employee admitted that he was behind on his rent and had made the cash advances on the credit card, but he promised he would pay them back. I did not find him genuinely remorseful. The tears he produced during this meeting appeared staged. We finished lunch and set up a meeting with him and the owner for later that day. During this meeting, the owner was upset, but the employee simply stared at him blankly, like a deer in headlights. Finally, the owner broke down and abruptly left the room. Still, the employee sat motionless and said nothing. When the owner returned and apologized for breaking down, the individual remained quiet. The owner took his employee's keys and credit card, told him to go home, and said that he needed to decide what he was going to do next. He told the individual not to come back to work until he heard from the owner. He advised the individual to start thinking about how he was going to repay the back rent, the credit card advances, and the loan.

The owner then asked his employee what he had to say about his actions. All the employee said was that he was sorry. However, he provided no further details, and there was no depth or emotion to his apology.

The owner terminated the employee. Subsequently, the owner did not receive any money from his former employee.

Later, a customer called the owner, requesting a statement for payments the customer had made during the previous year. The owner found no records in the accounting for the customer, so he requested that the customer provide copies of the front and back of their checks. The owner reviewed the copies and learned that the customer had made the checks payable to his employee rather than the business. The employee had then cashed the checks and kept the proceeds. The customer said he had also paid the employee once in cash. The owner was now learning why the business's profit was off $100,000 from the previous year. His employee had been stealing customer payments while the business paid the material and labor costs.

The owner said he'd lost faith in trusting anyone going forward. He decided to scale the business back to a manageable level so that he could run the business himself until he sold it off and retired. ▪

I have experienced cases where the victim wanted to meet with the person responsible for the fraud, so that they could ask them questions directly and hear first-hand what the person had to say about their behavior. I have also experienced cases where the suspect asked to meet with the victim, to explain in their own words what happened and to apologize. While these meetings never rose to the level of where the parties hugged at the end, I truly believe both parties benefited from facing the other person, in person, to clear the air and be heard.

In the cases where someone refused to meet, or was directed by counsel not to meet, even though closure was obtained over the fraudulent activity, closure never occurred for the emotional component of the case. Knowing this, to the extent possible where the safety of everyone involved can be assured, I have encouraged individuals involved in my matters to make a meeting happen, even if later it proved unsuccessful. If for no other reason, my client will forever know that at least they tried.

Hopefully, the fraud examiner realizes that setting the stage for managing client emotions is critical. In the next chapter, I discuss the personal actions a fraud examiner can take to increase their success in managing client emotions.

CHAPTER TEN

Managing Client Emotions

T HE PREVIOUS CHAPTER FOCUSED on you, the fraud examiner, and strategies you might implement to manage emotional clients during a fraud engagement. Part of my success in this area is due to my practice of discussing my approach with the client and attorney up front, prior to accepting an engagement, so that they are both fully informed about what my firm can do for them. In that discussion, I tell the client that I cannot guarantee what I will find as a result of our involvement or what will happen as a result of our findings. Those are things that neither I nor anyone else can predict or control. However, I tell the client that there are two things I can control in their matter: my interest in their case and my passion for resolving their matter.

Now I want to take the discussions to an even more personal level and share some recommendations for the fraud examiner to implement. By utilizing these strategies, the fraud examiner can minimize the emotional issues directed toward them and their work during an engagement.

TAKE AN INTEREST IN YOUR CLIENT'S CASE

A brief discussion about customer service is warranted here. In far too many transactions these days, the consumer is perceived as just another number. When I was growing up, customer service was emphasized and great customer experiences were expected. Sadly, today it seems that average or poor customer service is the norm. Many people nowadays focus on simply getting the product;

the level of customer service is less important. Take coffee drinkers, for example. Many individuals are willing to wait in long lines to get their specialty coffee made the way they like it and they pay a premium for it, regardless of how the servers treat them. These customers don't seem focused on how they're treated as long as the store continues to make the coffee they like. Coffee drinkers return day after day, regardless of how they are treated, until some other competing coffee shop opens nearby.

However, customer service is paramount in the context of fraud engagements. The fraud examiner is providing a service, and their client is the consumer. This analogy may be limited in some contexts – for example, when a fraud examiner is an employee within an organization – but in the context of my firm where referrals are our lifeline, great customer service is what keeps us in business. Individuals would not continue to use my firm if they were not treated well, since there are other fraud examiners who provide similar services.

We've had many clients come to our firm complaining that they've been working with another firm where they felt as if they were just another engagement. My firm's approach has always been different. Unless I've worked with an attorney or law firm in the past and had a positive experience with them, I rarely accept a new client engagement without setting up an initial meeting to meet the client and their attorney. (Owning a firm comes with benefits, one of which is choosing who you want to work with on engagements.) Before I decide to work with a client, I want to hear their story and see what facts have been discovered to date. I listen to the attorney's strategy for resolving the matter, and I get a sense of whether I want to work with the client. Before I get involved, I ensure that the client and their matter are the right fit for my firm, background, and experience. I provide great customer service, and I want to be sure that the client will appreciate my firm's work.

I tell clients that, while I cannot predict or control the outcome of their matter, I can control the experience they will have working with me and my firm. I tell them that I set certain expectations for myself and that these expectations also apply to my staff. When I accept a new engagement, the client won't be treated as just one of many cases we are working on. We take a personal interest in every matter, and we see it through until it is resolved. We track all our cases on a whiteboard in our office so that we can monitor each case throughout the process. We also provide regular updates to our clients. When we haven't heard anything about a case in some time, we reach out to clients and counsel to obtain a status update.

Many of our cases settle during the process, and clients and their attorneys don't always remember to let us know. However, when a case resolves through settlement or any other means, we want to be aware of the outcome. When a case is resolved, we don't simply archive the files and erase the case from our whiteboard. We want to know what happened, how the case was resolved, and what part our work played in reaching the resolution. This practice not only shows the client that we're interested in their case beyond the point of being paid for our services, but it also adds to our knowledge and experience, which we can draw on when resolving future matters. While not every client provides us with this information (and in some cases the settlement is confidential), most of our clients do, which helps us bring closure to the matter.

BE PASSIONATE AND GENUINE

Earlier in the book, I attributed much of my career success to two things: I care, and I'm passionate. If you're looking for advice on how to stand out in this field, I recommend two things: Be passionate about your work, and be genuinely invested in discovering what happened in every matter. Given unlimited time, resources, and access to records, a fraud examiner could of course pursue all avenues to seek out the truth. However, in reality, no one is ever given unlimited time, resources, and access in a case – but that doesn't mean you can't ask for everything that you need, knowing you likely won't receive it all. In my experience, clients recognize and respond favorably to the level of rigor you invest in resolving their matter. Taking an interest in their case and pursuing it passionately also helps when it comes time to collect payment from clients.

Just as people love great customer service but don't often find it, most people want to work with passionate people but rarely find them. You have complete control over how you approach your client matters. Decide to be the one to deliver both passion and superior customer service to your clients, and you will do well in this field.

PRACTICE WHAT YOU PREACH

Everyone has had experiences where they were promised the world and then were disappointed to receive less than they expected. Be realistic in setting your clients' expectations to ensure that you can deliver on your promises. Clients are watching to see if you actually do what you say you will, and they'll notice if you deviate from your word. Clients hold you accountable, so you need to be sure that your words and actions are consistent. If, for example, you said you would provide them with an update by Friday, you need to send them that update even if you don't have anything new to report. The client will be expecting your communication. A key strategy in managing client emotions is delivering what you said you would. If you do this consistently, you will find that more and more people want to work with you on future matters.

In one of the divorce cases I discussed earlier, you may remember that the target of our work in a divorce investigation call me "disingenuous." Since at that time I didn't know what the word meant, I looked it up on my phone as soon as I took a break from our meeting. I learned that the word meant "insincere" and "dishonest." The target of our investigation thought I was working with an agenda. I took offense to his statement because I had been entirely transparent with him about all my activities and why they were taking place. When our meeting resumed, I told this individual that I disagreed with his assessment. I told him that I had no hidden agenda and that I'd honestly told him everything I needed to do and why during the engagement.

He said he didn't believe me. I told him I couldn't control what he believed, but I had been honest and upfront with him the entire time. I told him that the only thing I could control is what I did and said; I could not control whether he believed me. Later in the case, I learned that he simply had a suspicious personality: He didn't believe anyone (perhaps it was because he himself was disingenuous). In any case, I was able to complete my work on the case without being triggered by his accusations because I knew that I had always been true to my word.

DON'T GET ATTACHED AND DON'T GET PULLED IN

While you need to show interest, passion, and sincerity in a client engagement, you must be careful not to allow yourself or a member of your staff to cross a line with a client. In certain situations, it can be easy to align with a client, to empathize with them so much that you allow their issues to become your issues. However, this is a line that you cannot cross as a fraud examiner. You have to remember that, while you care about helping your client, their issues are their own.

Maintaining this boundary can be difficult when a vulnerable client leans on you. Because you have listened to them and showed compassion, they may start to act as if the relationship has changed from professional to personal. If this happens, it's crucial for you to maintain a proper degree of professionalism and detachment in order to preserve the client relationship.

I have yet to come across one rigid set of criteria that ensures that a fraud examiner doesn't cross a line with a client; it's subjective to each client and each matter. It can be difficult to identify when clients are crossing lines, so you must remain vigilant. Here are a few warning signs to look out for. If a client becomes comfortable sharing information beyond the scope of the matter, asks for advice on personal issues, or requests to meet socially, the client has most likely blurred the distinction between professional and personal. If a client calls or texts without regard to your personal time, detailing personal issues or daily drama beyond the matter you are working to resolve, the client may be trying to draw you into their personal world. They are looking for someone with whom to commiserate.

In these instances, you must stop the client and reestablish boundaries and parameters. Otherwise, the client will continue along this path, ultimately taking the relationship into a personal arena – especially if you choose to ignore their communications. The client may say things like: "I thought you were more than a fraud examiner. I thought we were friends, and friends don't treat each other like this . . ." If such a scenario happens, you will have to address additional client emotions directed at you personally, which may create problems for you as you try to perform the services for which you were retained.

In my firm, I treat all clients with respect and empathy, but they do not become my friends, buddies, or travel companions.

In some rare cases, a client's interests may align with your own, and you may find that you enjoyed working with them on their matter. In those rare instances, you could explore a relationship beyond the professional, but that could only happen down the road after their matter has been resolved and your professional involvement has come to a conclusion.

I emphasize to my staff time and again: "Do not let the client's issues become your issues." I tell them to listen when the client calls, respond to their texts, and give them advice, but to keep things professional. If the client needs further support, direct them toward resources they have relied on in the past: family, friends, and business associates. While we want to be responsive in helping our clients resolve their matter, we should not become their sole resource in solving all their life's challenges.

 ## DON'T LET THEM MAKE YOU FEEL BAD

The fraud examiner's job is to do the best job possible for the client. The fraud examiner cannot control what information will be available, nor can they control who will be cooperative in meeting and providing information. The fraud examiner can control how clients are treated, and how responsive he or she is to client communications. However, the fraud examiner cannot control the outcome of the case, or the decisions made by the court.

Some clients will be unhappy with their outcomes and the costs incurred with their case. They will complain – and in some cases, complain a lot – but their level of complaining is also beyond the fraud examiner's control.

Too many times I have had staff tell me that they felt bad about the cost we had incurred on a matter or the outcome a client received. I have had to remind them that it wasn't our fault and that we should not feel bad. We did the best job possible, and that was all they asked of us. I tell them we should never feel like we did anything wrong, or that we had any role or responsibility in what happened to the client, because we didn't. We had nothing to do with what happened, so why should we feel bad? We were retained to try and help resolve whatever happened, and we kept the client and their attorney informed all along the way about our progress and the costs being incurred. That's all we can do.

TAKING A PERSONAL INTEREST VERSUS TAKING A CASE PERSONALLY

The standard I have set for myself and my staff is to take a personal interest in a client, care about their matter, and be passionate in performing our services. However, I make a distinction between personal interest and taking a matter personally.

To illustrate this divide, I will return to the very first client matter I discussed at the book's beginning, which involved a brother and sister resolving their mother's estate.

> As the brother and sister's case continued month after month with no clear sense of how and when it would be resolved, I received many texts, calls, and emails from our client, the sister. Each time a new issue arose in her case, she would become highly emotional and ask for advice on how to proceed. As you may recall, the sister and her brother had wanted to remove their stepfather, who had abused their mother, from the house their mother

had owned. However, because the court process is generally slow, holding the stepfather responsible and removing him from the premises proved to be no easy task.

Each time the sister contacted me, I would ask her how she was doing and listen to her response. The courts had intervened enough so that her stepfather's hemorrhaging of her mother's money had stopped, but the fact that her stepfather had not been held accountable for his actions made her alternately angry and depressed.

On one occasion, she became very depressed as she thought back on all the terrible things her stepfather had done to her mother, and she wished things had worked out differently. In a few days, she was scheduled to fly out of town and would not be back for a while. Knowing this, I went online and found a book for her to read on her plane journey. The book talked about how to accept what had happened, so she could process that these events hadn't been her fault and that she'd done the best she could with the information she'd had at the time. I sent her the book on overnight delivery because I wanted her to have it the next day. I also put a card in the envelope that stated I hoped she could find peace as her case worked toward resolution. Once I'd sent the book off, I told her to be on the lookout for some reading material I'd sent her to read while she was on the plane. She called the next day and said she was so grateful for the book and couldn't wait to read it. She also said she deeply appreciated our involvement in her mother's estate issues.

All it took to show this client that I cared was a $10 book, a quick note, and an overnight delivery. No tall tasks or major feats, just a small token to show her that someone cared. There is no magic to my formula for a successful career in this field – I just choose to care.

It is often easy to empathize with a client and the issues they are trying to resolve. Frequently, clients describe how they have been mistreated or have suffered. Many of their stories are heartbreaking, and you can't help but feel for them and their families. People can be very cruel to one another. However, you have to remind yourself of your role and work to set aside any biases you may have formed while listening to their stories. You have to remain objective. While you may have no reason to doubt what the client has just shared with you, you must remember that thus far you only have one side of the story. When you learn the other side, it could support the client's story or it could show that the client has been less than truthful. My approach is to listen to a client's story to learn their version of events and then seek out other versions (to the extent that is possible and practical). Often, the client's story contains puzzle pieces that I have had to piece together with other investigative work to determine what really happened.

Fraud examiners working on an engagement can cross a line when they allow biases to influence their outlook, approach, and strategy. Those biases may originate from the client's story. The following engagement provides an example of how bias can impact a fraud examiner's objectivity during a case.

At an initial meeting with me and my staff, a client going through a divorce described how her husband had been cheating on her with a younger woman, while leaving her home with their young children, with whom he never spent any time. She said that when he was at home he drank, used drugs, and physically and emotionally abused her and the children. He had spent their life savings on his lavish lifestyle with his girlfriend and had fully mortgaged their house. She was very emotional during the meeting and cried at times as she described how she'd struggled to feed her kids while he drove around in his sports car and dined at expensive restaurants.

After the meeting, I met with my staff and asked for their reactions. They were angry with the husband. I asked them why. They said it was because of the way he had treated his wife and kids. They said that only a monster would do that to his own family. I asked them why it mattered to them, and they said they felt bad for the woman. She deserved better. They said it wasn't fair how the husband had led a lavish lifestyle while leaving her home to care for their family. I told them, "That may well be true." I then asked them what any of those feelings had to do with the fraud procedures we had been asked to perform. Before they could respond, I told them it had nothing to do with our services. We had to approach every engagement objectively and without bias, and the results would be the results. I said, "If we approach an engagement any other way, then we will miss things or only look for things that support our desired outcome, and our objectivity will be impaired."

I told them that it was normal to feel badly for the woman and to think that the husband was a monster based on her description of him. However, we didn't know if those events had really happened or happened the way she described. Our role was to remain objective and perform the fraud procedures to the best of our abilities. We had to be indifferent as to how the matter was resolved, rather than hoping that our work would support an outcome we desired. ▪

Looking back on my fraud investigation experience, I can recall cases where I felt bad for the individuals involved, victims and suspects alike. I also remember plenty of individuals I disliked, for whom I performed procedures as best I could. Although I disliked these clients, I tried hard to not let that interfere with what I needed to do. In the end, to the extent that it's possible, fraud examiners must strive to remain independent, objective, and professional in our roles.

The fraud examiner must never get emotionally involved in a client matter. You cannot cry when your clients cry and get angry when they get angry. You have to remind yourself that the client's issues are not your fight and that you have no stake in the outcome. Once their fight becomes your fight and you start to take a position in the case, you have lost objectivity and your usefulness in resolving a matter diminishes, if not disappear entirely. Fraud examiners simply cannot get emotionally involved in the client's matter. I recommend that you be responsive, supportive, passionate, professional, and genuine, but that you never let your client's matter become your personal concern. As a fraud examiner, you should have no stake in the issue or the outcome.

If you are working with less experienced individuals on a matter, you should be vigilant about objectivity (or the lack of it). If your staff members are working on a client engagement, monitor and recognize when they may be headed down the slippery slope of emotional involvement. If that happens, you will need to intervene, bring the staff member back to an appropriate level of objectivity, or reassign them to a different client matter.

You also need to recognize when a client is trying to pull you in and make you more involved in their issue than is warranted. In those cases, you need to reestablish boundaries and reiterate your role in their matter. You must then ask that the client keep your relationship on a professional level.

It's important to maintain objectivity and impartiality in your approach, conduct, procedures, relationships, and communications, not only to maintain a professional relationship with clients but also because your behavior, if inappropriate, could be used by opposing counsel and parties to preclude you and your work from the case.

 ## UNEXPECTED EMOTIONS

When it comes to client emotions, be prepared to expect the unexpected. The details of fraud cases change frequently as unknown facts come to light and clients' emotions shift based on new developments or information. You should be prepared to address client emotions during every phase of a fraud engagement, including after a matter has been resolved.

Unexpected emotional interactions are not limited to clients but can arise with any individual involved in the matter, and you should expect these types of interactions from anyone involved in the case, regardless of their position or role. The more experience you gain in this area, the less surprised you will be when new emotions crop up.

The following story involves an unexpectedly emotional call we received from someone involved in one of our cases.

We received a frantic call from an administrative assistant working in a medical practice. She said a marshal had served her with a subpoena. The subpoena said that the administrative assistant would be deposed by an attorney who represented a coworker accused of stealing from the practice. The administrative assistant was panicking, talking a mile a minute. She said she wasn't available on the day the document said she needed to appear. And she had never been deposed before. She worried about the questions she would be asked and how she would answer them. If I had been able to measure her blood pressure at that moment, I imagine it would have been dangerously high.

I let her go on for a minute or so. When she stopped talking, I asked her to take a deep breath. I couldn't tell if she had done so, so I told her to take another breath so I could hear it. Then I asked her to listen for a minute. I told her that she needed to relax. We could talk about the deposition. I told her that the date could be moved and that there was time to prepare for the deposition. I reminded her that she was not the person who had stolen from the practice, so she didn't have anything to worry about. She needed to stop letting the news of the deposition disrupt her day and to put it out of her mind for the moment. I then explained what a deposition was and how it worked.

After a few minutes of her asking questions and me providing calm, easy-to-understand responses, she thanked me. She said that the marshal showing up had unnerved her. Crazy thoughts had started to race through her head, and she'd started wondering if she could end up in jail. I told her she was not the defendant accused of stealing; she was only a witness. She needed to remind herself that she hadn't done anything wrong and that, if her former coworker's attorney wanted to ask her questions, all she needed to do was answer them.

She thanked me, and I told her we would meet closer to the date of her deposition to go through it all again: how a deposition works and how to prepare for one. Until then, she should put the prospect of the deposition out of her mind. ▪

I'm glad I was in the office when she called. In as few as 15 minutes, I was able to calm her down, provide her with information she could understand, and turn her day around.

EMPATHY VERSUS SYMPATHY

A discussion about emotional involvement would be incomplete without discussing the difference between sympathy and empathy. In client matters, it is important to remain empathetic versus sympathetic. In simple terms, sympathy involves feeling sorry for someone, having pity on them. Empathy, in contrast, is about understanding how someone feels given the situation or scenario that they are in. When you feel empathy, you recognize and understand how the person must feel, but you do not pity them.

In my firm, I want my staff to treat clients with empathy. However, I don't want them to become sympathetic. I don't want them to feel sorry for the client, and I don't want the client's issues to make my staff feel bad. I want my staff to understand how the client feels and to show concern about those issues. However, staff need to draw the line to prevent having the client's issues become their own issues.

In the next chapter, I discuss how to react to emotional clients.

CHAPTER ELEVEN

Reacting to Client Emotions

TAKE THEIR CALL (AND THEY WILL CALL, AND CALL, AND CALL)

Just like you, I have often received calls from individuals I didn't want to speak to at that time – or didn't want to speak to at all. At times, I see a call come in from a potential client I spent far too long with on the phone the day before or a client who calls several times a day, every day. Sometimes I take the call just to answer the client's question and get them off the phone. Other times, I let the call go to voicemail, knowing that I'm simply deferring the inevitable: my need to call them back. If too many of these types of calls go to voicemail, I find that I later have to be on the phone for far too long as I return these messages, so I've developed a strategy to balance taking calls versus ignoring them.

In the calls I immediately take, I start out by setting expectations for how long I am available to speak. I may tell the client that I only have a few minutes and then I have to step into a meeting, participate in a conference call, or leave for an appointment. This strategy helps define for the client how long they have to ask me a question. If a client calls at the end of the day, I may tell them I have to leave at a certain time, but that I have a few minutes before that to speak with them. Setting expectations around time is important in creating clear boundaries. It also encourages clients to abbreviate their stories or questions.

While this strategy may not be the most helpful to use when starting a new engagement, it is definitely one to consider once the engagement is underway. I use a similar strategy when I return messages. I indicate at the very start of the conversation that I have a fixed amount of time to speak, after which I have another matter to address.

I have also learned that, when I'm on a call with someone who is being unreasonable or providing lengthy, unnecessary, or repetitious details, a break in the conversation proves invaluable. Stepping away from a conversation but promising to return to it provides an opportunity for the client to calm down (or they may even forget what it was they were ranting about). Just be sure you honor your commitment to call them back, even if you dread getting them back on the phone. Apply this same strategy to voicemail. After receiving an emotional voicemail from a client, wait a little while before calling them back. Chances are, if you let a little time pass between their message and your response, their emotional state will have changed or subsided in the meantime.

In times of crisis – and by "crisis," I mean when they are panicking about their case – clients call you. Even if they've already left you a voice message, they often call again. They might leave numerous voice messages about the same issue, all within minutes or hours of one another, and after that they'll still continue to call. If you're on another line, they may ask whomever answered the office phone to put them on hold so they can wait until you're off your call. Once on hold, they will grow impatient, hang up, and call back again. And so the cycle continues . . . unless you take steps to stop it.

Train staff members who answer your phone to tell clients who want to wait on hold that they're not certain how long you'll be on the phone. The staff member should then ask the caller to leave a message. If the caller has already been put through to your voicemail more than once, the staff member should tell the caller that you will receive their messages once you're available. No additional messages are necessary. If you don't limit the number of times a caller leaves a voicemail, you may find that they leave several messages, which you'll then spend the next 15 to 30 minutes listening to.

Although call management is important, you should make exceptions when a client calls with an urgent issue. If a client is in the midst of an emergency, I may interrupt a meeting to take their call or ask the person answering the phone to tell the client I'll call them immediately once I'm available.

Of course, what a client considers to be an emergency might be very different from your definition. My rule of thumb is this: "Fool me once, shame on you; fool me twice, shame on me." If a client's call turns out to be a truly urgent matter, then if they again call claiming there's an emergency, I react accordingly. However, if a client calls claiming their issue is an emergency and it turns out not to be urgent after all, then I will let future "emergencies" from the same client go to voicemail, where I can review their message at my convenience. My experience has been that the majority of "emergency" calls I receive are not of an urgent nature and can wait until I have time to respond.

However, when in doubt, if you can, take your client's call. This strategy minimizes the number of subsequent calls and voice messages you'll have to manage.

One last recommendation when it comes to phone calls and voice messages: Emotional individuals often leave extremely long voice messages, getting to their question or point only at the very end of the message. One way to address this problem is to ensure that the message duration in your voicemail system is limited. A shorter message duration forces callers to leave shorter messages before they run out of time and the system cuts them off.

There are a few drawbacks to this strategy, however. A very emotional client who runs into a message time limit might leave you several successive messages. Or, in an attempt to get all their information into a short message, callers might talk so fast that it's difficult for you to understand what they're saying. In those cases, you may have to listen to their messages several times, wasting precious minutes of your time.

Those risks aside, however, setting limits to voice message duration in general leads to shorter, more manageable messages from clients.

RESPOND TO EMAILS, EVEN WHEN THEY'RE LENGTHY

In this day and age, people tend to expect instant responses to their emails. Clients can grow frustrated when they don't receive an immediate reply to their emails. The challenges of email are similar to the challenges of voice messages, but clients are more prone to abuse email due to the ease with which they can send them. An emotional client can quickly send you multiple emails about the same issue, perhaps several times a day. They can also mark their emails "urgent" and then expect instantaneous responses to their communication. I believe that clients who use email on their mobile devices and respond to emails even in the midst of other activities expect that everyone else also accesses and responds to emails in the same way. That is simply not the case. I don't receive or send emails on my mobile devices; I only use my office and home office computers to read and respond to emails. I mention this fact in my expectation-setting session at the inception of every engagement, and I tell clients not to expect immediate responses to emails, as I am often in the field and unable to respond until I'm back in front of a computer.

Once you've dealt with a client's expectations around email responses, you will still have to deal with the content of their emails. When emotional clients are alone and have time to think about their case, they tend to write emails – and some of these emails may be the longest ones you will ever receive. If you were to print these emails, they would span pages and pages. The client may also include various pictures and documents, some or all of which you may have previously received and reviewed.

One strategy I use to handle lengthy emails is to limit my response to them. My replies to these emails are short but meaningful. For example, if a client emails me a long, detailed rehash of the same information I've previously received, I don't ignore their email. Rather, I choose to respond, but I limit my response to just a few words, such as, "Received. Thanks for your email." By doing so, I ensure that the client knows I received and reviewed their communication, hopefully precluding them from sending follow-up emails.

LET THE CLIENT VENT

Victims of fraud, just like any other victims of crime, find themselves dealing with a wide spectrum of emotions. As a fraud examiner, you have to provide a calming influence and listening ear. You must be their voice of reason. You may find you're the only person in a matter who cares about the individuals involved and provides an open channel for the client to talk.

Many past clients have described their experience of their fraud matter as an emotional rollercoaster. Stress affects people in different ways, and someone under stress can be lucid one moment and out of control the next. Clients have told me that, during their matter, they felt in control one day but panicked the next.

Over the course of my career, I have received many calls, voice messages, and emails from highly emotional clients who were very angry. When I first started out in this field, I got angry myself at these calls and messages – and my mood was probably apparent in how I dealt with clients. I remember feeling affronted. I had done nothing to upset these clients, so why were they treating me this way, as if their issue was my fault? In my head, I put them on a virtual list of clients I didn't care to ever speak with again.

The following story demonstrates how emotional clients may direct their emotions at the nearest available target: you.

Early in my career, I went to a women's medical practice to help with some of its accounting issues. I had never met this client before; I was simply covering for another accountant at my firm. I hadn't been provided any background information on the client, so I didn't know anything about the issues they were facing. When I arrived at the practice, I realized I was the only male in the waiting area. Once I was escorted back into the offices and examination room areas, I realized I was the only man in the entire place. A tall, middle-aged female doctor, one of the practice owners, brought me into an office and, for the next 15 minutes, screamed at me about all of their bookkeeping issues, their lack of information, and anything else she could think of. She was so loud that another staff member closed her door for her. I knew this doctor was directing her hostility at me simply because I happened to be an available target.

All I could do was listen, since I had no background information about the case and hence couldn't counter anything she was saying. When she finished her tirade, I asked her why she was so angry with me. I had never been to her practice before, and I had nothing to do with any past issues with the accounting. I told her I would address any issues she had identified, but that she first needed to tell me what those issues were.

At that, she left me alone in the office and never returned. In her absence, I reconciled the practice's bank accounts and reviewed the transactions within the system as best I could. Then I asked a staff member to find the practice owner to see if she wanted me to address anything else. The owner never returned, so I left. I can still remember how I felt, heading down the hallways toward the exit: as if I was undertaking a walk of shame. Everyone I passed knew I had been the one the doctor had yelled at. She'd made me feel inadequate.

When I returned to my firm, I shared my experience with the firm's partner and the accountant whose client I had met. Neither was fazed by my story or how I'd been treated. I ended up being sent to the medical practice office at a later date, during which I addressed all of the issues they had identified for me. They must have been impressed with my work, because I was assigned to the practice after that. The doctor I'd initially met with at the practice never yelled at me again; however, she also never apologized for how she had treated me on my first visit. ▪

People in general are under a lot of stress, and everyone has bad days from time to time. When you add a fraud matter to the mix, people's stress levels only increase and some individuals can snap under the pressure. What I eventually came to realize is that I needed to retain my equilibrium even when those around me were losing theirs. Now, I remind myself that I do the best job possible on these matters. I am more responsive to issues than most; I keep clients informed and updated better than most; I am passionate; and I care. If I happen to do something wrong during an engagement, I own it. I don't make excuses or try to deflect blame; I address the issue immediately. Thus, if a client calls and is angry, yells, screams, or behaves in a hostile manner, I realize that their emotions likely have nothing to do with me; more likely, they are reacting to something else going on in their lives. They've simply chosen to vent their frustrations on me.

Rather than reacting emotionally, I let them vent. I don't try to stop them, and I don't try to respond. I just let them go on. I may take notes during their tirade, or I may just listen. I have found that eventually the client has to stop and take a breath. I have yet to encounter someone who continued their rant indefinitely. That's not to say that if the client becomes abusive or vulgar I let them continue. However, in most cases, I've found that the most effective technique is to let the client express themselves.

If they are upset, I let them cry. If they are angry, I let them yell. If they are frustrated, I try to explain things to them as best I can. However, I remember that I often have little control over the source of their frustration – for instance, the speed with which their matter gets resolved.

If your client appears unappreciative of your work, don't become upset. Remind the client that you are trying to help them resolve their matter. Acknowledge that you are frustrated by the same things they are – for example, an unresponsive attorney or a delayed court date. The client will thank you for all of your efforts, and then – most likely – will later call and yell at you about something else. This behavior is par for the course. Clients will flip-flop, act irrationally, and appreciate you one day and then unleash their anger on you the next.

My advice: Let the client do all of those things. In my experience, it is merely part of the process. Fraud examiners have no control over their clients' emotions. All you can do is react to them and try to help them when possible. The following story illustrates the way fraud examiners have to retain their emotional equilibrium, even when dealing with highly reactive clients.

When I worked at a public accounting firm, one of my areas of expertise was selecting and implementing accounting systems for small businesses. At this time, personal computers were becoming popular and automated bookkeeping systems were becoming prevalent.

My firm had a client who ran a local shopping plaza. He was retired from the military and was very structured in his approach to life. Although he wasn't my client, I became aware of him because of stories I heard from others in our office. By all accounts, he was not a pleasant person, and he often yelled at the accountants who worked on his account.

At one point, a partner sold him on the idea of buying a computer and automating his bookkeeping. He agreed, and – since I was the implementation expert – I scheduled a time to meet with him. His bookkeeping needs were relatively simple: tracking monthly rent payments from less than a dozen commercial tenants and recording the expenses associated with the plaza. It was very easy to set up his system and show him how to use it. After he'd entered a couple dozen transactions, he seemed to get the hang of it. I added the program to his desktop menu and watched him open and close the application several times to ensure he was all set. I left thinking I'd done a good job.

The next day, the man called me at the office and started screaming at me. He wanted to know why he'd paid so much for a computer program and my services when he didn't even know how to use the darn thing. When he'd finished with his tantrum, I asked him what had changed from the time I'd left him yesterday. He said he'd turned his computer off, and when he turned it on that morning, everything had been different. I couldn't understand what he was talking about, so I drove over to his office to see what he was experiencing.

When I got there, I asked him to walk me though his issue. He showed me where he always went on his computer menu to shut down the computer. Then he showed me how he'd put a disk into the disk drive to keep it clean overnight, as he did every night. He said when he turned the computer on that morning as he always did, everything on his computer had been different.

I noticed there was a disk still in the computer's disk drive. I asked the client if he always kept the disk in the drive, or if he removed it before he turned on his computer each day. He said he took it out and only used it to keep dust out of the drive. I then asked him why this disk was still in the disk drive this morning.

That's when the man realized his mistake – he'd booted up the computer with the disk in the drive rather than with it removed. A very humbled client opened the drive and removed the disk, then shut down his computer. When he restarted it – *voilà!* – the menu was there on the screen along with the accounting program. He clicked on the bookkeeping system and could access it just as he had the previous day. I asked him if he had any further questions, and he said he didn't. I thanked him for meeting with me, and I left.

Truth be told, I wanted to clobber this client for yelling at me, but I simply let it go. Did I think this client was a jerk? Certainly. No one should be treated the way he'd treated me. But did this client know that I thought he was a jerk? Absolutely not. ▪

In this story, the client was unfamiliar with technology and upset at how much the accounting system had cost him. In addition, he was frustrated that he couldn't figure out the system on his own. These are understandable feelings. However, his over-the-top reaction was unwarranted. He probably just wanted to vent his feelings – perhaps about the accounting system, or perhaps about other things in his life I wasn't aware of.

RECOGNIZE THAT CLIENT EMOTIONS ARE NOT ABOUT YOU

If you work in this field long enough, you will realize that the emotions directed at you during an engagement are never really about you. You just happen to be in the wrong place at the wrong time (or, from the client's perspective, in the right place at the right time). After the client's matter is resolved, you will often receive warm expressions of appreciation from people who were previously difficult, abrasive, and even hostile.

In many cases, after a client exploded with emotion during an engagement, they've subsequently apologized to me. Many are embarrassed by their behavior and say that their conduct was not a reflection of who they normally are. Nearly all of them say that their rant had nothing to do with me personally, but rather was an expression of their frustration or anger about their case.

If you work in this field, you have to expect to deal with highly stressed individuals whose behavior may be erratic. Although I don't intend to be a punching bag for clients, I also recognize that there will be times when clients need to let off steam. When this occurs, I try not to judge them and I work hard to remind myself of how people act under stress, which can be very different than how they act in normal circumstances.

REMIND THE CLIENT TO BREATHE

When clients are highly emotional, they sometimes forget to breathe. Once they've got you on the phone, they talk without interruption, seemingly without taking a breath. They tend to be all worked up about some issue in their matter, perhaps an issue you've discussed with them several times before. You have to find an opportune time when they pause to remind them to breathe: tell them to take a deep breath, let it out slowly, and then take another. I tell both my clients and my ambulance patients to stop and breathe during stressful situations. Oxygen does wonders for the brain and the mind. Taking a few slow, deep, cleansing breaths gives the client a few seconds to pause – and also allows you to digest what they've been saying.

I've used this strategy for over 25 years in my work on the ambulance. When I arrive on a scene, individuals are often panicking. Once I establish that the person's issue is not life-threatening, I recognize that there is no great hurry to their matter – so I slow things down and tell them to breathe. Many times, I tell them to breathe again, and then again. This technique has a calming effect. Once I have the person calmed, I can figure out what has happened and get them where they need to go. When I arrive on a scene, the patient's pulse may be at 150, their breathing at 20, and their blood pressure 150 over 100. Once they've taken several deep, calming breaths, their pulse drops to 80, their breathing to 12, and their blood pressure to within normal limits.

Most crises in fraud engagements are similar, with the main difference being that fraud is usually not a matter of life and death. Most people simply need to calm down enough to figure out the logical next steps in their case. However, since the issues may seem like life or death to your client, you will need to provide a voice of reason for them.

When a client calls or meets me and I can see that they are emotionally overwrought, I let them vent and then I tell them to breathe. If I'm on a phone call, I ask them to breathe loudly enough so I can hear it from my end. I use this directive in part as a psychological tactic. Focusing on their breathing distracts them from their emotions just long enough to provide me an opening to start reasoning with them. I then identify what exactly has them all worked up.

The following story shows how it may be necessary to calm and soothe an individual in a matter so you can proceed with the necessary next steps.

We were engaged by an attorney to assist with taking over an entity's operations by court order. Having completed similar engagements in the past, we knew that these abrupt takeovers often come with all sorts of emotional and sometimes physical reactions from those at the targeted entity.

We arrived unannounced at a business and waited in the hallway outside the door until the first person arrived for work. Once the first person arrived, the attorney announced our intentions, shared the court order, and proceeded through the unlocked door into the business. Needless to say, this woman was taken aback and began to panic. We told her to have a seat in the conference room, and we sat with her while the attorney and others secured the business.

We asked the woman where the owner of the business was that morning. She said he had gone to an early appointment and would be in later. We explained to her that we would be securing the business, computers, and all other information we needed. Repeatedly, she asked why this was happening. However, all we could tell her was that the court had ordered the attorney to take control of the business.

The more time that passed, the more overwrought she became. We had to sit with her and remind her to take long, deep breaths. We told her we understood that this situation was sudden and unsettling. We told her we would stay with her as things settled down, and then we would identify a systematic approach for her to identify the files and information we needed to locate. In the meantime, other staff members worked with the attorney to photograph and videotape the office spaces before anything was changed. ▪

You have to expect people in your cases to become emotional. When that happens, you will likely be the one to calm them down, simply by telling them to breathe and relax and by answering their most pressing questions.

When you meet with a client in person, you can make light of the situation and add levity to a heavy, stressful meeting. Take a break, stretch your legs, raise your arms over your head, and take long, deep breaths. All these actions can help interrupt a stressful meeting and restore a sense of calm – especially when a meeting involves both a suspect and a victim. These meetings can be especially draining for everyone involved. During them, it's critical to recognize when the parties need a break. Even a simple bathroom break can be helpful, since it allows individuals to step away from the meeting and gives them time to stand, stretch, and talk amongst themselves.

Here's another technique I've learned: distraction. Distracting a client during an emotional crisis can work very well in alleviating heavy emotions. In the following case, I had to use distraction to manage my client's growing anger.

We were retained by the attorney representing one of two business owners involved in a business dispute. Our client worked out in the field, interacting with clients and bringing in business, while the other individual worked in an administrative and financial role, collecting fees, depositing funds, and paying the bills.

The company had done very well, and cash flows had never been an issue. However, at some point our client learned that his partner may have been using business funds for personal activities. Some of the business's revenue, which was stored in a safe located onsite at the business, was no longer there.

The owners' relationship deteriorated, and the owner who ran the office ended up changing the locks, essentially locking our client out of the business. Both individuals retained counsel, and litigation ensued. We were retained to review the business's financial activity, to determine whether the partner had in fact used funds for personal purposes. The partner refused to make the business records available, making our job even harder. However, we eventually proved that our client's partner had withdrawn several hundred thousand dollars from the business without our client's knowledge.

Needless to say, our client was outraged and felt deeply hostile toward his former partner and friend. We held several meetings, and in each one, the two came close to a physical altercation. The attorneys agreed to settle the case through mediation, and a judge was selected to perform the mediation.

During the settlement discussions, our client got angrier and angrier at his former partner. As the morning progressed into the afternoon, our client lost his cool to the point where he began to swear in front of the judge. The judge listened as I presented my findings, and he seemed to agree with the direction the settlement needed to go – against my client's partner.

Once the judge left the room to talk with the partner, I reminded my client that he needed to keep his emotions in check. He couldn't forget that he was meeting with a judge – he needed to stop swearing and lashing out. He agreed to do better when the judge returned, but I knew that he would have a tough time with it.

Then I remembered that it had been some time since we had taken a break and that he, like everyone else, was likely getting thirsty and experiencing low blood sugar levels. I found a bag of peanut M&Ms in my backpack and offered them to him. He was appreciative. That snack, coupled with a water bottle, seemed to return him to a more balanced state of mind.

The judge returned and shared that he had obtained the settlement agreement from the other owner and that we should meet as a group one last time to sign it. When the other owner came into the room, he sat across from our client. He noticed our client eating M&Ms and asked if he could have some. My client smiled from ear to ear and said no. Then he continued to eat the M&Ms, one at a time, in a very deliberate fashion.

Justice and closure, when and if it happens, appears in different forms for different people. ■

Psychology and client intervention – although not well-documented within the growing wealth of materials relating to fraud examinations – play a very large role in this field. As a fraud examiner, you will benefit from seeking out more training in these areas.

SET A TIME FOR CLIENTS TO LISTEN

During an engagement, it's important to set aside time when you get to talk and clients must listen. After my clients have vented about their issues, I always ask them if it is my turn to talk now. Then I tell them I understand their feelings. I try to address their issues, one at a time, keeping them calm as I provide my responses. If they try to interrupt me, I calmly stop them and remind them that it is my turn to talk. I have been courteous enough to listen to them without interrupting, and I now I'm asking for the same courtesy from them. I tell clients I will allow them to ask questions once I have finished talking.

In situations like this, most clients let me talk. However, if they don't, I suggest that we reschedule our conversation for another time. On a very few occasions, when the person has simply been out of control, I've tried several times to interrupt their ranting, to no avail. In those cases, I've warned the client two or three times that I am going to end the meeting or call if they can't get themselves under control. In cases where they have persisted, I've simply had to hang up or leave the meeting. This reaction is not one I resort to often, but it's necessary sometimes. I cannot reason with an unstable person.

The same protocol holds true for emails. If an unreasonable client continues to bombard you with highly emotional emails, even after you've repeatedly asked them to stop, send them an email that warns them that if they persist, you will block their emails and stop responding to them. If they persist, do as you promised. However, after some time has passed, you may review their subsequent emails. If it appears they have returned to acting reasonably, you can then reinstate their email access.

RELAX, CLEAR YOUR MIND, DECIDE WHAT TO DO, AND BREATHE . . .

When a client contacts you and it's clear that they are worked up, recognize their emotional state and let them express themselves. Then begin to talk them off the ledge. I find this is easier to do on the phone than over email. If clients send you a long email and you respond with an email of your own, you will likely become drawn into a lengthy email exchange. I find it's better to pick up the phone and call the client. Once I understand their issue and have calmed them down enough for a reasonable conversation to take place, I ask them what they need from me. Many times, I've asked this question only to have a client say that there is nothing they need from me; they just needed to talk about their issue with someone. In my experience, these types of calls are easy ones. Although at first the call is emotionally draining and requires my full attention, I later realize that there is nothing I need to do in response. There are no procedures to perform, no tasks to complete. Many clients just want to talk to someone who understands their case and the process they're going through.

 ## WRITE IT ALL DOWN

Clients often have a lot of questions about the process of investigating a fraud matter, as well as questions for the individual who committed the fraud. During the pendency of an engagement, the client's list of issues will circulate in their head, creating emotional issues for them until their matter has been resolved. Even after a matter concludes, their issues may remain unresolved, as key questions can go unanswered. The client may never get the opportunity to find the answers that can bring them closure.

I tell clients to write down their thoughts in as much detail as possible, to get the information that is swirling around in their head down onto paper. Many clients who have followed my advice have told me that this exercise was very therapeutic. Writing down their thoughts helps clear their mind and helps them not to dwell on open issues and unanswered questions. Their writing can be useful in other ways as well. They can provide written questions to their attorney to pose to the suspect at deposition or trial. In one recent case, I asked a physician who was the victim of an embezzlement scheme to write out all the questions she wanted to ask the perpetrator. The doctor produced 29 pages' worth of questions.

 ## FOCUS CLIENTS: KEEP THEIR EYES ON THE PRIZE

When a client decides to initiate a case, they identify goals and outcomes they want to reach as a result of the investigation. However, over time, delays and unexpected developments can overshadow these goals as the client becomes bogged down by distractions. Procedural measures, counterclaims, and information requests can make a client feel as if they are the one being punished, rather than the perpetrator. The process can shift a client's focus from pursuing restitution to defending themselves against attacks. In some extreme cases, this effect is intentional; the opposing side bombards the client with requests and attacks to dissuade them from further pursuing their matter.

Most clients have never been through anything like this process before. They need assurance that things are proceeding as normal and that the requests and other procedural measures are all part of the process. Request that your client forward you copies of any requests, letters, subpoenas, or other communications they receive so you can review and explain them. Clients do have attorneys who can advise them on any documents they receive, but most experienced fraud professionals also understand the process very well and may be able to better explain it in layman's terms. Reviewing copies of these documents also allows you to remain up to date on how the case is proceeding. In addition, you can identify procedural measures that may be excessive, abusive, or simply impractical. Communicating your observations to the client's attorney proves helpful, especially if you have reviewed these materials in advance of the attorney.

When the going gets tough in a fraud matter, remind the client of the goals they are working toward. For example, if the client wants the perpetrator to go to jail, then they have to pursue the case criminally. After law enforcement is involved and the perpetrator arrested, then the fraud victim's wait begins. The defendant may postpone their scheduled court dates and cause delays month after month. However, in the end, the case will come up on the docket and get resolved, either through a plea deal or through a trial. Advise clients to register with victim services, and request that victim services send them regular updates via email. By doing so, the client can minimize the risk that they'll show up for a scheduled court date only to learn that the court date has been postponed.

Holding a fraud perpetrator accountable is possible, but it takes a while to complete the process. Remind your clients that patience and persistence are essential in resolving a matter.

REMIND CLIENTS TO CONTINUE LIVING THEIR LIVES

Anyone who has been involved in a fraud examination and the ensuing criminal and civil processes knows that these matters take quite some time to resolve. It's not unusual for a case to span many months and sometimes years. While the case is pending, clients unfamiliar with the process get frustrated that things are not happening quickly enough. You will need to let them know that it's common for a case to stall during a phase of the investigation or legal process, further delaying the ultimate resolution. When a case is significantly delayed, the client often starts to regret ever beginning the process and loses hope that their case will get resolved. Unfortunately, the wheels of justice turn slowly, and financial matters take time to resolve. Fraud cases are difficult to detect and complicated to explain, and unfortunately they take a lower priority than other types of legal cases. The justice system has limited resources, and if those resources are consumed with other matters, a client's case can be significantly delayed.

Clients often call asking for progress updates on their matter, even when they know you don't have any new information to share. Recognize that they are feeling frustrated, talk to them, and remind them that although the process moves slowly, it does move. Often, I take the initiative in calling the different people involved in a case and asking for updates, making sure that the case is not forgotten. As the saying goes, "The squeaky wheel gets the grease." I stay on top of my open matters and provide regular updates to clients, and I find that this practice reduces the number of calls I get from anxious clients.

When a client is frustrated or regrets initiating an engagement, I remind them of the initial goals they set for the investigation. I remind them that financial crimes, unlike other crimes, rarely result in an immediate arrest and speedy trial. The client is doing the right thing in holding the perpetrator accountable. They should feel proud that they chose to investigate rather than passively accept their loss. I then assure them that their case will be resolved, even if it takes a long time. Open cases do not stay on the court docket in perpetuity.

In the meantime, I tell the client to move on with their life and return to what matters most to them – family, friends, business, health, hobbies, interests, and, most of all, happiness. Once their case is in process, there is nothing more for them to do but wait. Rather than dwell on the case, they now need to move on. When the time comes that the case is ready to be resolved, the client can then refocus on the details of the matter. Until then, they should set it aside and go back to living their life.

CHAPTER TWELVE

Final Thoughts

I F YOU ARE LIKE me, you usually have a busy schedule, with more going on at any given point than you have time for. For people like us, deciding to read a book is a major investment of our scarce time, especially if you read slowly like myself.

Hopefully, you have found it worthwhile to read about the information I've shared in this book. My goal here has not been to author the fraud field's authoritative guide on emotions, but rather simply to share insight, experiences, strategies, and techniques.

I have been fortunate enough to have assisted clients and attorneys in fraud and financial matters for 31 years. My career experiences have allowed me to start and run my own boutique fraud firm for the past 16 years. I have been further blessed to have been asked to teach fraud examination and forensic accounting at the University of Connecticut School of Business's Master of Science in Accounting (MSA) program, as well as Manchester Community College's continuing education program.

I will now tell you what I tell all of my students at the end of every semester. If you want to succeed in your field, in whatever career you choose, you need to do one thing and do it very well: Be passionate. This credo has worked for me in all my undertakings, and I trust it will work for you as well. Set the bar high, and surpass expectations.

I wish each of you much success in your professional and personal endeavors – and make sure to set aside time for yourself to enjoy the ride along the way. Good luck, and stay well.

Index